CHEAPEST IN THE END

CHEAPEST
IN THE END

By Madeleine Bingham

DODD, MEAD & COMPANY ❧ *NEW YORK*

Library of Congress Catalog Card Number: 63-17440

Printed in the United States of America
by Vail-Ballou Press, Inc., Binghamton, N. Y.

Contents

CHEAPEST IN THE END

1 ❧ ❧ ❧

A Beginning

I AM not a novelist. I have had novels published, but then so have a great many other people who are not novelists.

This book should have been a play. Three acts which would move to laughter and tears. It was to have been a picture of a man and his family, and how they lived in a past that is dead, from the twenties to the fifties.

But then the thought of all those actors getting older and older, with Wigs by Wig Creations, and Wheelchairs by the Old Times Furnishing Company, mildly depressed me.

A book?

Not another family saga. I would not deliberately choose to wade into the deep morass of family-saga writing, unless I needed the money really badly.

Social significance? In my record, there could be none. We were not rich, we were not poor. Unlike our dynamic modern writers, I am not a believer in class significance. I believe only in people, good, bad, and indifferent.

I wanted to write of people. The people who surrounded me

when I was young. And I wanted to write out of affection.

Why not, then, quite simply write the truth?

The pointillist painters built up a sunny landscape with a series of dots of color. Surely that is exactly how the life of a family is built? Little dots of color, scarlet, black, shimmering blue and rose. A landscape painted in this way could give the complicated threads of joy and sorrow, of laughter, of anger, and of affection which form the life of a family.

Most families are undistinguished. So was mine. Most fathers lack grand forebears, or ancestral acres. So did mine. Many fathers leave their children nothing when they die. Mine left me nothing.

Well, not exactly nothing. A few things, a chair, a dish, a Persian rug, some maps, a picture . . .

Every family has "things," things which are kept for the recollections which they bring. Some of them are worth keeping, even perhaps a little valuable. Then people say, "I do hope that Mother isn't going to leave that nice gilt clock to Alfred." Some are quite pointless, even embarrassing; then people say, "I do wish Mother would get rid of that terrible motto on the drawing-room wall."

This is the record of an undistinguished man and the things which he left me, things which would not fetch a hundred pounds under the auctioneer's hammer.

The worth of a man's life lies in the ideas which he leaves in the hearts of those closest to him. I think my father left us two things, a sense of family, and a sense of home.

Some of the most trite phrases in the world have been written about home. People looking back on their childhood exaggerate either its horrors or its grandeurs. I hope that I have not fallen into these errors.

Basically it doesn't matter whether one's home is that of an antique dealer's daughter as mine was, and furnished in excellent taste, or whether it's tea-shop Tudor with gnomes. If my father's garden had had a gnome, it would be outside my window now.

A sense of home is a sense of security. It is a solid basis in a bleak world. A raft to swim back to when the ship has sunk.

If you have been fortunate enough to have had a happy childhood, it doesn't matter how the pattern changes. Probably you may not be able to give your children the things you had yourself.

Your house may be smaller, more cramped. The rug which looked so elegant on polished oak floor in the country may look drab in a London villa.

But through disappointments, disasters, difficulties, and death, a sense of home is always in your heart.

2 ❧❧❧

The Ham Knife

THE ham knife is long and slim, very slim because it has been sharpened these twenty-five years. It has a black handle and a hook to hang it up. It is never hung up. It is not often used to cut a ham. But it is a link with a past when hams in the larder were not such an uncommon occurrence.

My father was very fond of food. There are those who knew him who will say that this is an understatement. While his appetite was good, food for him also had an aesthetic appeal. He did not mind if food was plain or fancy. It was all the same to him so long as it was good.

A nice round Stilton at Christmas, a capon specially dressed from the butcher's, vast pyramids of fruit in the dining room, all these had for him an equal appeal. He liked the look of them. For him they had the same artistic satisfaction as similar piles of food for the Flemish school who painted them. He just appreciated the look of a well-stocked larder. It was like the first bars of a symphony to a music lover.

A richly growing vegetable garden also moved him to a feeling of the poetry of growing, harvesting, and eating.

My mother was extremely uninterested in food, and her one wish when he was on holiday or at home at week-ends was to prevent "Clemmy going shopping."

I remember her wails of protest when the car door opened and the back was seen to be full of melons, pineapples, special lardy cakes, parcels containing slices of *pâté maison,* thick cuts of gammon, and whole cheeses.

"He doesn't seem to understand," she would complain to me, as the eldest and most responsible child, "that whatever he buys they will eat."

This statement contained the complete dichotomy of their views about food. My father's idea was to fill the house with good things, to invite people in to share them, to see his children round the table having second helpings of everything. This gave him real pleasure.

There it was, the groaning board. His four children waiting expectantly. A large joint on the sideboard, with surrounding vegetables and sauces. This was the kind of thing he liked. He would raise his knife, and the feast was under way.

My mother's idea on food was quite different. Her aim was to make it last, to eke it out, and be economical with it. She had no sympathy at all with my father's lavish Tudor attitude towards it. Food was to keep body and soul together.

"Your mother doesn't take food seriously," said my father to me sadly one day, and then conspiratorially he added: "You and I will go shopping, eh?"

To go shopping for food with my father was just the thing any child would enjoy. There was no female haggling over large or small cauliflowers. No argy-bargy about the value of melons or pineapples.

The sight of a greengrocer's shop was for my father like the clarion call of the huntsman's horn to the hounds. There it all was. Colorful, beautiful, on sale, and ready to be carried away.

Women, I used to think when I was a child, always do such dull shopping, half a pound of sago, a tin of Vim, and don't-forget-the-self-raising-flour. Men, on the other hand, just order things to be carried out to the car. They indicate the largest bunch of grapes nestling in its cotton wool, they don't worry if it is "just over the two pounds." They like the look of the whole bunch, no mean snipping to bring it down to "under the pound." Bags of nuts are bought to look pretty and fill in the cracks between oranges. Bananas are bought by the bunch—no question of tearing them off and spoiling the ship for a hap'orth of tar.

Not that my father ever admitted that he was extravagant. Far from it. When he was accused of extravagance, a hurt look passed over his handsome features.

"It's much cheaper," he would reply, with a tone of finality, "to buy a decent amount. What is the use of these piddling little economies, half a pound of this, and a quarter of that?"

No one ever answered this rhetorical question. My mother continued to economize during the week, while my father went on wonderful week-end shopping sprees. When my father had been on a shopping expedition the larder had the look of a marvelous cornucopia. Shelves overflowed, tables were covered with parcels, and often there was not enough room to take the bags and boxes which emerged from the car at the kitchen door.

As children we enjoyed all this, because the obvious thing

6

to do to save shelf space was to eat everything as speedily as possible. This infuriated my mother, who used to hurry off hiding grapes, melons, and nuts in cupboards in the dining room, or in high-up hidey-holes in the kitchen.

When we sat down to table my father would look around.

"Where's the box of peaches I bought?"

"I'm keeping them," said my mother.

"They were bought to be eaten," said my father.

"We'll have them on Monday," she replied.

"But they were just perfect for eating today," said my father.

His French blood could not bear the idea of peaches being put away just when he had bought them for eating at that precise moment. They were *au point*. Each one had been selected by an appreciative Gallic finger. There was no question of putting these gems away till Monday. Monday! Such an idea would occur only to a woman who had no real appreciation of food. The peaches would be produced and consumed.

Whatever he bought my father liked to buy in good solid quantities. Quantities which were at once apparent. He had friends in the food business who abetted this attitude. When I sent for jam from school, it came by the case, twenty-four assorted pots of jams in different flavors. If I wrote for sweets, I would receive two large boxes of assorted toffees and mixed sweets. When I say large boxes I don't mean the kind of boxes which one buys privately in a sweet shop, I mean the six- or seven-pound boxes from which the shopman serves the sweets out. It took me a long time to get through those boxes of sweets because in my convent we were only allowed sweets on Sundays.

Christmas was the time my father enjoyed most. It was then he could give full rein to his feeling for food. Turkeys, geese, chickens, whole Stilton cheeses, boxes of chocolates, *marrons glacés,* Metz fruits, Carlsbad plums, all the traditional fare was supplied in lavish profusion. Fortunately, Christmas was not a time to be given over to "piddling economies."

The thing my father liked best at Christmas was the excuse to buy a whole ham—"cheapest in the end," of course. He loved to carve a ham, and was very good at it. Everything he did, he liked to do with artistry. He told me that he had learned to carve by watching a man in a cooked-meat shop when he was a very small boy.

"It all depends on the way you start the ham," said my father. "If you go wrong at the beginning, the thing is spoilt."

To watch my father carving, or doing anything else which required delicacy, was always a pleasant experience. It is good to see things well done.

When we were small, and even when we were older, each plateful of meat was a separate problem. Judith, being the smallest, would have a little very thinly carved beef, no fat, a little of the red gravy, and Nanny could cut it up, but not too small, because, as my father pointed out, the flavor would be spoiled.

My mother liked a little fat, but not too much, and my brother would have a slice of the outside because he liked it better cooked. These were problems not to be lightly glossed over.

Food was a serious subject.

Just before the last war my father built a house near Chichester Harbor and we used to spend all our week-ends and holidays there. It was a wonderful excuse for the buying of provisions. On the night we arrived my father would produce three or four pounds of steak, tomatoes, mushrooms, and bags full of fruit and cheese.

"We will do the real shopping in Chichester tomorrow," he would say. He thought of this meal as a light snack. The serious business of real shopping could be undertaken the next day.

Chichester, before the war, was not a busy place. There were still old-fashioned shops, and chain stores had not yet filled High Street. It was just the kind of place which my father liked for shopping. There were little bakers tucked away which still made homemade bread, and nice warm doughnuts could be bought. Heavy plum cakes could be found. Above all, there was a marvelous cooked-meat shop, and outside there swung a golden ham.

"There you are," said my father one day. "That's just the sort of shop you used to be able to find in London when I was a boy. A real old-fashioned cooked-meat shop."

He looked delightedly at the bow window and the swinging golden ham. I could see that the swinging sign was soon to be converted into reality.

We waited at the counter. So many good things. Cheeses, pickles, *pâtés,* good old-fashioned homemade sausages, none of this manufactured stuff full of bread. This was the proper way to buy food. My father looked round with artistic satisfaction.

There they were on the counter. Beautifully cooked hams, breadcrumbed, rosy, the fat just right.

The shopman approached, his red face beaming. In his hand was a long, slim, ham knife. He was ready to ply it to the satisfaction of his customers.

"What can I do for you, sir?"

"I want a ham," said my father.

"Which ham shall I cut from?" asked the man, eyeing his wares appreciatively.

"I want a whole ham—to take away."

The man, used to women shoppers asking for a quarter of a pound of ham with no fat, hardly blinked an eyelid.

"Yes, sir, what weight would you be wanting?"

"I don't mind," said my father, "so long as it's a good ham, and well cooked."

He gave the shopman a shrewd summing-up look. The two men eyed one another. They both realized that they were in the presence of equals. Men who cared about hams. There was to be no messing about. It was the whole ham or nothing.

"You could, of course, take the small well-cooked ham," said the shopman, and he reached up a long tentative hook towards the ceiling. My father's expression seemed to tell him that the small well-cooked ham was not perhaps quite good enough.

"Or again," said the ham seller, "we have the large half-ham. You then get the sweet meat near the knuckle, but not so much of the milder more fatty meat."

My father considered the half-ham. The shopman hooked it down. They both contemplated it.

"Cheaper, of course, near the knuckle end," said the ham man.

This was an error. Cheapness was not the thing my father was looking for.

"I wasn't thinking about the price," said my father reflectively.

The ham seller realized that he was in the presence of a man who considered hams, not as food, but as a means of artistic satisfaction and contemplation.

"In that case—" Expectancy filled the air as he raised his hook, and this time he swung down a wonderfully large bread-crumbed ham. He put it on the counter.

Again they both contemplated it.

"Well-matured," said the ham man.

My father looked at it. He didn't intend to appear too enthusiastic.

"Fatty enough, but not too fatty," added the ham man in dulcet tones.

Still my father gave no sign of being really baited with the ham man's hook.

"Of course, it may be a bit large for you—it must weigh all of fourteen pounds."

This was the right approach. To suggest to my father when he was out shopping a smaller size, an economy, a "piddling economy," was a challenge.

"I could cut it in half," said the ham man.

My father's aesthetic instinct was aroused. He looked at the ham. Sadness filled his tones.

"That would be a crime."

After a little bargaining on price, with give-and-take on both sides, the ham was wrapped.

My father paid in crisp new notes. It was one of his fads never to use dirty notes. If anyone gave him a dirty note, he either spent it very quickly or took it back to the bank.

Just before my father picked up the ham he turned to the shopman. They smiled at one another. My father looked at the white china ham stand which stood on the counter.

"How much do you want for the ham stand and your ham knife?"

"Well, sir, those are not for sale."

"I know," said my father, brushing aside this fact as irrelevant. "But how much do you want for them?"

A price was agreed and we added the ham knife and the ham stand to our purchases and left the shop. The ham was reverently placed on the back seat of the Buick, and we drove off down the Birdham straight to Itchenor.

"He's bought a ham," I said to my mother as we went into the kitchen.

"We shall be eating it for weeks!"

"Not the way he makes ham sandwiches for picnics," I said.

It was decided that the ham would be started for lunch. A large salad was made. My father was very fussy about salads and always mixed them at the table himself. The way his father had taught him when he was young. Once the salad was mixed my father started the carving ceremony.

The ham was reverently placed on the ham stand. The ham knife was sharpened so that it would cut the proverbial hair, and the meal began. At least we all thought it had begun. The knife sliced into the ham.

When the ham man had spoken of the ham being "well-matured" he had not exaggerated. The ham was so well matured that it was crawling. The old-fashioned shop had been just that little bit too old-fashioned—it had no fridge.

My father gave a howl of baffled rage. It was the despair of someone whose cherished dreams have been shattered. It was not that his meal had been interrupted, it was that the crowning achievement of the purchase of his ham, the actual carving of it, had dissolved into anticlimax. Hamlet had tripped over one of the floats.

THE HAM KNIFE

He snatched the tablecloth from the side table, and tied the ham up in it as one would tie up a bundle of washing.

"Come on," he said to me, "you were with me when I bought it. We're going back!"

With the ham on the back seat we drove into Chichester at eighty miles an hour. Fortunately for my father the lunchtime traffic was not heavy in those days, for he was a fearsome driver. The best plan was to shut one's eyes and pray to St. Christopher, because if one kept one's eyes open one had the feeling that even a saint could not save one.

Ham, with maggots, sat on the back seat, like an accusing figure shrouded in white linen.

"Everyone takes me for a bloody fool," growled my father. "I may be a fool, but I'm not a bloody fool."

As no one in their senses would ever have treated my father as a fool, this statement, which he frequently made, had an air of fantasy about it which we children used to giggle at nervously, and not within my father's hearing.

We arrived at Chichester. We pulled up at the old-fashioned hamshop.

"Pick up the ham," commanded my father. I did so, and we went into the hamshop.

My father did not speak. I laid the well-matured ham down on the counter.

"Look!" he said to the ham seller.

The ham man looked with acute dismay and embarrassment at the ham. He could not deny the evidence of his own eyes. He folded the tablecloth reverently round the well-matured ham and took it away to be cremated quietly.

My father did not speak. He did not believe in long speeches.

He just liked service.

The ham man came back from the obsequies of the ham.

"Would you accept another ham," he said in a quiet, sad voice.

"If you think it is safe," said my father.

He did not believe in pressing further points about the ham. The man was prepared to make amends, and once his point had been accepted he was prepared to be magnanimous.

"This one was cooked only today," said the ham man, "only today. It weighs sixteen pounds, and you can have it for the same money."

My father's expression did not weaken.

"You have been inconvenienced," said the ham man.

"I have. I was just about to start lunch."

Possibly the ham man realized the enormity of my father being stopped in mid-flight towards a square meal. I don't know. He leaned towards my father.

"Would you accept two pounds of this delicious Stilton? It's in perfect condition," added the ham man in the sad tones of an artist about to give away a cherished canvas.

"I would," said my father.

The sixteen-pound ham was wrapped. The two pounds of cheese was wrapped. My father with a grim expression accepted the tribute and left the shop.

I gave the ham man an extremely tentative smile, which he did not notice. His blue eyes were fixed on my father as he stumped out of the shop. He followed us to the door.

My father laid the ham on the back seat, he put the cheese beside it, and he gave a dismissing nod in the direction of the ham man.

THE HAM KNIFE

"Everybody takes me for a bloody fool," said my father, furiously slamming the heavy door of the Buick.

I looked back at the ham man. He was nodding and smiling nervously. The slam of the car door made the golden ham swing on its chains. We shot off round the Cross at a furious speed. The level-crossing gates were shut. My father slammed on his brakes, the sacred ham fell off the back seat.

I didn't like to tell my father. Perhaps I would be able to hustle it into the house without him seeing.

So that's why we still have the ham knife in the kitchen drawer, although we very seldom have a ham.

My father had an artist's eye for food; it was not greed for eating which inspired this attitude. His father came from Strasbourg, the home of *pâté de foie gras;* possibly this aesthetic feeling for food was in his blood. He liked to be surrounded by good things, good things to look at, and good things to eat. The best was always only just good enough for him and for his family.

Perhaps it was that touch of *foie gras* in the blood which made him what he was.

3 ✄ ✄ ✄

The Limoges Dish

HEREDITY is enchantment. When the child is taken to the church to be baptized and anointed, and the salt is put on his tongue, around the font gather the shades of those who have gone before. Like ghostly godmothers and godfathers, they confer blessings and burdens. A shapely mouth, a vile temper, even the lines on a hand, or a way of laughing without restraint. There are no ordinary families. Every family is strange and varied. Like plants in an untended garden, "sports" are rampant. There is no pattern. Anyone may turn into anything.

My father was born the son of a French refugee from Strasbourg. His mother was the pious daughter of a businessman living in Soho Square. She became piously converted to Catholicism. She went to Mass in the French church in Soho, which was how she came to marry a French refugee. My grandfather left Alsace about the time of the 1870 war. The family was scattered. Whether as a result of some grim family tragedy, as my father suspected, or merely because their land was overrun, I have never discovered.

THE LIMOGES DISH

A portrait of my grandmother's father hangs in our house. Not well painted, the picture shows a prosperous Victorian with heavy-lidded eyes and bulging shirt-front. Tradition has it that he kept a large establishment in Soho Square, ran a carriage and horses, and died leaving very little money. Photographs prove that my father inherited his heavy-lidded eyes.

Families tend to forget their history. Stories are handed down by word of mouth. And unless the stories are funny or tragic, they are often forgotten. Families go up and down. They lose touch with one another. The middle classes are specialists in ups-and-downs because their status is so often based on the ability of their individual members. My father's forebears were not only middle-class in two countries, they were also specialists in ups-and-downs.

My father, the last of the three children of Jacques, the French refugee, and Amelia, the pious daughter of the Soho businessman, was born in 1880. He was born on September 8, which is celebrated as the birthday of Our Lady. On this account, he was baptized Clement Mary. Not really a terribly good idea, when you happen to live in England. Marie, although quite current as a name for boys in France, was an embarrassment in England. But then my grandmother had not the faintest trace of humor in her make-up. She, like so many converts, exaggerated her Catholicism.

A couple of days with my grandmother could turn anyone into a freethinker.

My father's family lived in a large house in Sydenham. I have driven through the district, and although it has gone down in the world, it still has an air of Victorian respectability and spaciousness. My grandmother didn't believe in "pigging it" in a small house. Status had a good deal more to it in those days than it has now, and it was easy to sink in Victorian times. Things could easily become "beneath you." As far as I can make out, a small house was "beneath" my grandmother. Perhaps she remembered the former glories of Soho Square, and the carriage and pair.

There was only one trouble to a large house. My French grandfather was not very good at making money. His business was that of a shoemaking Lobb, but devoted only to the making of handmade evening pumps. Those were the days of the specialist, and under his supervision were made the soft patent leather and *glacé* kid shoes, with silk linings in pale blue, crimson or white, emblazoned in gold thread with crests and initials, worn by the nobility and gentry. I have seen shops which still make them, and I have even seen a retired general wearing them after dinner in his country house. Perhaps my French grandfather was too much of a perfectionist. Maybe he allowed his men to work too long and delicately on the shoes, but profits were hard to come by.

His lack of success made him a dim cipher in his own family. His wife called him by his surname, which does not seem to indicate either a deep or richly lasting affection. My grandmother had three children in three years, and then retired from the maternity business. Possibly she thought sex overrated. The Victorians were happily reticent about their intimate secrets.

When my grandmother retreated from maternity, my grandfather retreated into his hobby, which was history. Most of his spare time was passed in reading heavy tomes in French and in German and playing chess with the priest. His speciality was French history, which he knew in the minutest detail. Family history relates that he knew the line-up of all the regiments in Napoleon's battles, how they advanced and retreated, and their losses and battle honors.

He hated England and all things English. Whether this was because he was not a success, or whether he found himself in an alien environment which did not suit him, I don't know. However, like many refugees, he contented himself with speaking English very badly, and grumbling. He never went back to France.

My grandfather's business is no longer in Soho. He went broke and died in 1916.

Jacques seems to have been a misfit. Probably a man who ought to have worked in a university, but through adverse circumstances found himself in the wrong environment. Possibly my grandmother married a handsome foreigner, only to find herself tied to a stranger with whose interests she had neither sympathy nor understanding. The late Victorian age was materialist in the extreme, and cash was treated with the greatest consideration and respect. People who had it merited consideration and respect only in proportion to their cash.

My grandmother, daughter of the heavy-lidded gentleman whose picture hangs in our house, was perhaps disappointed in her bargain. Marriage is a terrible lottery. She had expected prosperity, and all she got was a list of Napoleon's marshals.

She does not seem to have been a very domesticated woman. Fortunately for her, in those far-off days there always seemed to be loads of cousins, spinster aunts, and odd females known as "poor Maude" who filled the gap in the families of ladies who were not disposed to be domesticated. Disappointed in the prowess of her husband in the business sphere, my grandmother took herself and her artistic talents out of the home, and became a kind of interior decorator to the Empire Theatre. She ordered and saw to the opulent flower arrangements of the period, she suggested the decorations and furnishings. She seems to have been a cross between a *fin de siècle* Constance Spry and a modern interior decorator. What she thought of the kind of promiscuous business to which the promenade of the old Empire Theatre was often given over, history does not record.

As I remember her, in the twenties, she was a large woman with masses of fine curling white hair, a mouth which was large and lacking in firmness, and enormous gray eyes. In her youth she must have been a fine woman, the kind of woman who sometimes appears in Victorian illustrations, sailing like some schooner billowing before the wind.

She rather overdid the church-going, was sometimes over-festooned with priests, arranged flowers in church, and made lace for albs, which are the long white garments worn by priests. So I do not need to stress again that she was very pious. One day, seeing me dressed up as Sherlock Holmes with a tweed cap, black moustache and magnifying glass, she solemnly evinced the sentiment that "Madeleine does not look very pretty."

In his family, my father seems to have been the odd man out. His mother spoiled his handsome elder brother, and made his sister her companion. Invitations were showered on the two older children.

Catholics, and especially Catholics who were half foreign, were not popular at that time. In the eighties and nineties, when my father went to school, they were often stoned by small boys as they went into the Roman Catholic school.

THE LIMOGES DISH

Possibly it was these delicate attentions from his Protestant compatriots, combined with his lowly status in the family, which made my father aggressively determined to get on in the world.

He grew into an extremely handsome young man. I remember seeing a picture of him when he was twenty-one. He had the glossy good looks of a *jeune premier* of the period. Patent-leather-black hair, a curving mouth, and large expressive eyes. This and his quick lively imagination were the only assets he had to start out in the world. His father could do nothing for him. Jacques could do nothing for himself.

When he was about eighteen my father seems to have gone through a stage of being an angry young man. On leaving the house one day in his salubrious suburb, his sister, entertaining friends, called out to him.

"Are you going to the office, Clem?"

"No, I'm going to work."

He always liked to call a spade a shovel. The ladies in the drawing room in 1898 did not appreciate his frankness.

My father's first idea was to get into the Navy. He had an uncle in the Zouaves, which perhaps gave him the idea of adventure and escape. I remember my father describing his uncle to me. His eyes flashed as he remembered the magnificent desert uniform.

"He was called Ment," said my father. "I'm called Clem; that's the difference between the emphasis in English and French."

It was impossible in those days for a boy without friends or influence to aspire to climb into the top or even medium rungs of the Navy. The way was barred.

CHEAPEST IN THE END

So my father took stock of his assets, and decided that he needed some outstanding skill. He had no accuracy, figures bored him. He had already been sacked as a clerk. So he went off to Pitman's to learn the new shorthand. He learned it with some success. He wrote 180 words a minute, and on the strength of this and his good looks, he got a job as personal assistant to an American businessman.

I can remember my father's shorthand. It looked exactly like a page out of Pitman's manual. He thought shorthand was good fun. I found this depressing. He could also read it upside down, and was apt to lean over his secretary's book and tell her she had made a wrong outline. He never did things by halves.

In his spare time, he perfected his French so that he spoke it without error, and without accent. He was a glutton for work, and whatever he did was done with the utmost skill and enthusiasm, except routine jobs. He hated routine.

The American taught my father the art of selling in business. It was a new idea in the early nineteen hundreds. My father was fascinated by business, and was quite determined to use it as a weapon to change his circumstances. He fancied being a managing director. In 1902 he met my mother. She was not averse to his being a managing director, either.

Opposites are so often attracted, and my parents were very much a team of opposites. Where she was quick and lively, he was slow-thinking and logical, pondering before he spoke. Where she had a sharp, lively, Irish, satirical sense of humor, he appreciated a profound thought well worked out.

Like my grandparents, my parents met at a Catholic dance. "Yes," said my mother reminiscently, "rose-pink taffeta with fine, fine, pin-tucking and slight train with ruching."

THE LIMOGES DISH

Like my grandmother, my mother was a convert to Catholicism; unlike my grandmother, she never overdid it. She has been known to hide in the coal cellar when a priest she particularly disliked called at the house.

I think my mother was attracted to the idea of being a New Woman. Certainly she had a bicycle and went cycling in Battersea Park with skirts above her ankles. And when her own mother died, my mother decided that she, too, was going to learn shorthand and get a job. She found staying at home dull. There was only one snag about her going off to Pitman's College —my father was also there. While she was prepared to accept my father's attentions as a long-term policy, she was not prepared to forego the attention of other young gentlemen who might amuse her. She said my father was her cousin.

There was not much love lost between my mother and my grandmother. Possibly my grandmother took a poor view of young ladies who bicycled in Battersea Park. Possibly my grandmother was one of those women who, unable to make a go of their marriages, become aggressively maternal. For, by this time, my French grandfather seems to have faded into the middle distance. A very distant figure in the family landscape.

Such stories as come out of the past do not seem to include my French grandfather at all. They show my grandmother, in elegant brocade, presiding over a houseful of young people. Her house, according to my mother, was always full.

"But when you provide food," said my mother, "it's astonishing how soon you can collect people to eat it."

There were supper parties, and impromptu entertainments of all kinds. And amongst the crowd of young people was the lively Irish Lottie, my mother. I can imagine that the quick, dark, bright girl did not look a good proposition to my grand-mother. Humor is a destructive force. Also, no owner likes to see a promising colt snatched from the stable. My father, mak-ing progress in business, seemed to have improved his family status by the early nineteen hundreds. His mother was now disposed to take a good view of him. Also, she was having trouble with his brother. Circumstances alter cases.

"The supper parties were fun," said my mother reminiscently, "but they also had musical evenings. The singing was very nasty. But the food made up for it."

She went on to describe the elegance of the flower arrange-ments, and the interesting kinds of meats and salads provided.

"I think the old man used to get a good deal of the food in Soho," said my mother vaguely. "And, of course, they had nice silver and very handsome china, Limoges, I think it was."

My French grandfather must have had very good taste. I still have part of the dinner service he bought when he married my grandmother. Every Christmas we carve our turkey on a large pink Limoges dish. The center is decorated with hand-somely florid blue convolvulus. Once the dish was ornamented with lavish gilding, but now nearly a century of washing-up has faded its splendor. There is something about that dish which deserves, and gets, a very large turkey. I don't know why, per-haps it remembers the supper parties of long ago.

Heredity is a strange thing. A year or two ago I went to a family funeral. It was a cheerful funeral; the deceased was eighty-five, so there was no actual cause for alarm. I saw a vague cousin of mine, a large Anglo-Saxon man with fair hair and a reddish face. Beside him in the car was his son. A hand-some young man, with delicately chiseled features, and black

patent-leather hair, and large expressive dark eyes. You could
have put him down in any boulevard café from Paris to Mar-
seilles, and he would not have looked out of place. I think
Jacques, the shoemaker refugee, must have looked like that,
which is probably why my grandmother married him.

My daughter, descended from a long line of Binghams, looks
like one of their forebears. But the thing she likes to do on a
Saturday morning is to go down to Soho for *pâté maison,* corn
salad, and Boursault cheese. She says English food gets so boring. Heredity is a funny thing. Quirky, really.

4 ❧ ❧ ❧

The Bow-Fronted Chest

BECAUSE the best was only just good enough for my father, "the best is cheapest in the end," was an accepted axiom in our family. It was my father's favorite saying. It encompassed everything from the purchase of a packet of cigarettes to the booking of a hotel room.

From the point of view of any bank manager, my parents did not make a good team. My mother had been brought up to be frugal, but when she had experienced my father's extravagance, she did not see why she should economize if he didn't. This meant that if he bought a new car when he didn't need one, she had a fur coat. If he spent too much money on the garden, she spent too much money on the house.

"I always remember my first lesson in extravagance," said my mother. "It was when I was in Paris on my honeymoon; I was trying on hats. I couldn't make up my mind between one in stitched satin, and one with ostrich feathers. Your father said to me, 'Why not have both?' I was astonished. I couldn't believe my ears."

THE BOW-FRONTED CHEST

"What did you do?"

"I had both, of course."

She continued to do just that.

The fact that my father's business was that of an interior decorator did not help. Ten or even twenty per cent off was still expensive when the job was done by a top decorator.

The house was always full of "men." They weren't the kind of men one sees around now, wearing jeans and with shaggy hair, leaving a mess behind when they leave. They were extremely suave craftsmen. They arrived wearing black coats and striped trousers. If they were cabinetmakers, they had all their stains and tools in a specially-made box of hinged mahogany. They asked politely if they might melt their glue in the kitchen. They were used to working amongst Top People and they had the dignity of their job. Head painters arrived for consultations like surgeons; they brought boards in variously tinted colors. They tested the feelings of the patient about colors. They conceded that my mother was happier with the russet tones, and then added a little yellow.

My mother enjoyed all this. And so did my father, until the bill came in. Then sparks flew. How could my mother have possibly spent three hundred pounds on nothing but men's time? Getting more and more angry, he would read out the details from innumerable sheets of thick golden foolscap.

"Men's time ten pounds, men's time five pounds, men's time eight pounds!"

Each time the repetition was like a hammer blow. Explanations were forthcoming. This had fallen off, that needed mending, there was a light to put up, another to be taken down.

"Haven't I told you *not* to keep on sending for *men?*" said my father.

My mother did not reply. She felt that the whole thing was extremely unreasonable. The men were available, and jobs wanted doing. What else could he expect?

My father's office was also a temptation.

It was full of wonderful antique furniture. In those far-off days it was arranged in alcoves, each one decorated in a different style. There was a Spanish alcove, with old leather furniture, and stiff antique copes in crimson silk on the wall. There was a Georgian alcove in pale blue silk with delicate moldings, and elegant Sheraton furniture. Upstairs there was an Adam room —the walls a pale Adam green, the carpet a brilliant emerald, and all the furniture upholstered in different shades of green and violet silk. To go to my father's office you went through an Elizabethan alcove, all old oak, pewter, and linenfold paneling. The paneling was a false door, and when you pushed it open you found yourself in my father's office, which was a lovely Georgian room.

He looked handsome and suitable behind his Georgian desk. Everything in the room was chosen with care; even the fireplace was elegantly Adam.

It is not difficult to realize that, given my parents' large-scale ideas, and surrounded as they were by all the elegancies set out for the titillation of the palates of the very rich, the result was they themselves spent too much on decorating at home. Things get to looking shabby pretty quickly when you are in the decorating business.

There was a great vogue for Tudor in the late twenties. So my father bought a Tudor house. My mother was doubtful about it. It looked rather large, and was too far from the station.

THE BOW-FRONTED CHEST

My father brushed all these difficulties aside. He had a fancy for Tudor. So Tudor it was. He sold his other house, we took our usual house at the sea for the summer, and my father got to work.

Armies of workmen camped out in the house. They pulled down walls, they relaid floors, they painted, they laid carpets, they scraped, they polished, and they set up a canteen in the kitchen. It was all costing a pretty penny. But that was for the future.

Meanwhile, my mother and father were happily engaged in finding furniture to fit the house. Old oak chests, rare oak cupboards with brass hinges—everything had to be in period. It's not such a simple job as you might think, moving into an old house. At least, not when you are in the decorating business.

Our original drawing-room furniture was only saved by a narrow squeak. If there hadn't been two sitting rooms in the house, that would have gone too. It was saved, but it was generally agreed that it didn't look right.

The house was lovely. It was a wonderful feeling, after a long walk in the winter woods, to come home through the falling dusk and to see the firelight flickering through the windows, lighting up the warm rich colors of the rooms inside. The tea was laid. Toast, crumpets, jam, perhaps even banana sandwiches. You looked into the windows at the polished oak and the familiar pictures. It was like a stage set which was awaiting the players, and yet a set which already had a heart. A heart which was a sense of home.

The Tudor house was a real home. It had drifts of daffodils in the spring, it had clouds of sweet-smelling lilac in May, roses and borders bloomed in June, dahlias flamed in October, and in winter the house was full of pots of chrysanthemums grown by the gardener, in the greenhouse. At Christmas he decorated the stairs traditionally with ivy and holly.

There was only one snag. The stock market crashed. And if there is one thing about the decorating business, it's the first to take the knock of a slump, and the last to recover.

After four years we moved. My mother was quite right. The house was both too expensive and much too far from the station. Anyone else might think that being too far from the station was just a small inconvenience. In our family it turned out to be expensive as well because we then needed two cars.

The new house was a hybrid; it was a modern house in an old garden. The original house had been burnt down. My father didn't really like the modern house. But tastes were already changing in the thirties, and Tudor was on the wane. He thought he could make something of the new house. To start with he didn't like the idea of a porch, and the hall was too small. So he took the front of the house off and knocked the porch into the hall. That made a difference. It was then a very large hall. So he bought a large rose-colored Persian carpet. That made it look "furnished."

There was something wrong with the drawing room. So he knocked a large French window in that.

Once it was lighter, the paint seemed all wrong. So the gentlemen in bowler hats arrived with their colored boards. Consultations took place.

We were, of course, living in our usual house at the sea again. This time at Brighton. Consultations went on taking place. None of the carpets or curtains was any good. Taste was changing anyway.

THE BOW-FRONTED CHEST

"It will make the move much easier," said my mother, "if we do away with all the old carpets and curtains. We can have the house absolutely ready, except for the furniture."

It made the move much easier. You could say it made it more expensive.

The new house, when it was finished, was quite as nice as the old one. It was gay, bright with color and flowers. The garden, although it hadn't got woods and fields attached to it, was over two acres of terraced lawns, and it was surrounded by clipped yew hedges in the shape of peacocks and spheres.

There were quite a few improvements to be done in the garden, too, but those could be done after we moved in. Everyone felt that we were well on the way to economizing.

After we had been in the new house a year, I got married. It was suggested to my father that we might have a quiet wedding, but he wouldn't hear of it. He said he rather fancied gilt chairs on the lawn. There was no budging him. He saw the whole thing. The garden would be a very good setting for a wedding, and it was.

"Men" were ordered. This time from Gunters. They came dressed like the craftsmen from the office, in black bowlers and striped trousers, carrying little attaché cases. They looked very curious, walking down the lane in the bright summer sunshine, like little dark spots of town life, set down in the country.

So my father had his gilt chairs on the lawn, and very nice they looked, too. There was no economizing about the wedding either. As he said, "the best is cheapest in the end."

A couple of years after I married, my mother decided that everyone spent far too much time in London. It meant that she was left alone at home, with no one but my grandfather,

Nanny, Judith, the maid, the gardener, and my father coming home early in the evenings and at week-ends, and others of us coming at the week-ends, too. Anyone could see that that was a lonely life.

I think the truth was that she now rather fancied a town life. There seemed to be quite a lot going on in town.

Also, my father was not very sociable. He felt that his family was all he wanted. And he didn't see why they should want anything else either. He was quite happy at home, and they ought to share his feelings. The fact was that my father was not very good "county," or even country, material. His capacity for finding dolts, fools, and snobs everywhere was illimitable.

My mother had fancies for learning bridge, joining the golf club, or taking up social work. She would have liked to have entertained and been entertained, but my father got very impatient. He met these chaps in the train, and most of them, he had already decided, were fools, or snobs, and in some cases both. He had no reason to believe that their wives would be any better. In fact, if he chanced his arm, they might even turn out to be worse.

The fact that he had no social pretensions was not a good angle in such a community. In those days Sussex was much more countrified than it is now. But already it trembled on the brink of the stockbroker belt. My father was not prepared to pretend that he was county, or to do anything because it was the thing to do. If his younger daughter rode, it was because she liked it, and not so that he could talk about "havin' a pony in the paddock." If he lived in a big house, it was simply because he liked big houses. If we currently had only one maid instead of two, he was not disposed to call her the "cook."

THE BOW-FRONTED CHEST

It is not surprising that my father had very few friends. People without social pretensions are always in short supply, and in Sussex, in the thirties, there were not many about. So he concentrated on his business, his family, and his home.

He was very satisfied with his home. Peaceful, comfortable, a nice garden outside, the scent of roses. He liked to put his feet up on the drawing-room settee and hear the bees humming outside. The French windows were open, he could hear the lawn mower. Things were very pleasant.

This mood of peace was not to last. My mother found him indoors once too often, sleeping on a sunny afternoon.

This was the excuse. What was the point of having an expensive garden kept up by an expensive gardener if my father was going to sleep indoors on a fine afternoon? Everyone was always up in London—Mark was up in London, Suzanne was up in London—that was obviously the place to live.

My father put up a stiff fight for the house. He put up a stiff fight for the garden. He clapped an impossible price on the property.

But it was met—on condition he sell the Persian carpet in the hall. The price was so high it was tempting. He sold the house and took a flat in London.

It was really rather an inexpensive flat, just near his office in Sloane Street. No train fares, no traveling, no gardener. It was fantastic what a great deal of money they were all going to save.

Of course, the country furniture looked all wrong in town. There was something about oak which looked dingy in London. London needed the richness of mahogany. The despised mahogany drawing-room furniture came back into its own. The green Chinese silk with the little pagodas was approved.

33

But the dining room would have to go. The hall would have to go. The oak bedroom would have to go. It was all stored.

The dining room, under the careful eye of the little men in the striped trousers, became eighteenth century. Changing taste transformed my mother's bedroom into French crackle-painted furniture, with chintz. Touches of russet, of course—she was "happier with the russet tones."

It was about this time that my brother took up sailing. My mother thought this was a very good idea. It would give him an outlet. Take his mind off women. He was nineteen, and had given no inkling of being overinterested in women, but my mother was taking no chances.

So my father took a house at Itchenor for the summer and bought my brother a boat. While he was down there, it occurred to my father that it was rather senseless taking furnished houses. It would be much better to buy or build a house. It would do for week-ends. Everyone would be able to come down for holidays.

So he looked round for a house. None of them seemed exactly right. They were either too small, or too ramshackle. He bought a piece of land. It was a very flat, wind-blown piece of land. It hadn't even a tree on it. Something would have to be done about that. He would get out a plan for improving it.

The landscape gardeners were very helpful.

They suggested a sunken rose garden, curving borders, a rockery, a little waterfall running into a small fish pond, a croquet lawn, hedges, a few trees at the other side of the house, shrubs round the drive—it all seemed extremely sensible, and would give the piece of land some character.

He decided to have the lot.

THE BOW-FRONTED CHEST

The house was built. There was, of course, no sense in having the cheapest bricks, or the cheapest finish to the house walls. The kind of little stones which sparkled in the sun made the best finish—they not only looked better, but they would last. The same thing applied to the drive. There was absolutely no point in economizing on that either.

The oak furniture would come in handy. It would look just right in the country again. It was a good thing it hadn't been sold. There were, of course, new carpets and curtains to be bought, and it was no good economizing on the kitchen equipment.

The house came out a little more expensive than the estimates in the end. But it was very attractive for all that. The garden was bright with flowers. There was only one snag—the hedges were terribly small, but time would cure that.

My brother's boat also turned out to be too small and too slow. Like my father, he liked to have the best. My brother consulted the men at the boat yard, he made inquiries—the only place to have a Sharpie built was Holland. My father agreed. My brother had also found out that the only place to get sails was at Uffa Fox. My father was in absolute agreement. There was no sense in economizing on sails once you had a good boat.

The bow-fronted chest is now in the dressing room. I bought it at my father's shop. We called it the shop, though my father used to laugh and say that his men preferred to say the "galleries."

It's rather a nice chest, with little ivory inlays round the keyholes, and a tulip design in rosewood down the sides. I was a little hesitant about buying it as we hadn't much money at the time. I wanted to buy a much plainer chest which hadn't these little refinements. We stood in the "galleries," my father and I, looking at the two chests of drawers. One gleamed with a depth of color, its bow-front threw back reflections. The other one seemed to dwindle under my father's eye. He looked at the bow-fronted chest with admiration.

"That one's a gentleman," he said.

The point was made. The sale was clinched. I bought the expensive one—less ten per cent. The best is always cheapest in the end.

5   ❧ ❧ ❧

The Maps

My father's attitude about always getting the best in life also extended to wars. He did not intend to let World War I get him down. Once he had decided to get into it, he decided to do it properly. And doing it properly did not include being a private.

He did not feel that his temperament was suited to being a private. Besides, he was already in his thirties. He felt he needed a little dignity. He had no influence, but this did not worry him. He made a few inquiries and joined the Inns of Court Regiment.

Those were the days when the Army was the Army, and those outside it were soon made to feel what outsiders they were. They were also the days of the horse. Once you put the combination of the insiders, who knew how to ride, against the outsiders, who did not know how to ride, you had a situation which gave good scope for interesting local oppressions.

My father was an outsider, and he knew nothing about horses. But one thing he did know—he wasn't letting anyone get him down. The combination of sergeant major and horse did not intimidate my father.

"I'd see the swine in hell first before I fell off," he said.

Because he was older than most cadets, my father was eventually sent into the much despised Royal Army Service Corps. It was a horse-drawn R. A. S. C.

The sergeants were only concerned with putting the fear of God into the recruits. They had devised a neat device for achieving this. The recruits were made to ride round and round a small arena with a team of horses and with a gun carriage trailing behind. Things were happily arranged by older and wiser hands so that, if the cornering was bad, the limbers of the gun carriage lifted the rider straight off his horse. Falls were many and bad. My father did not fall off. It took more than a horse or a sergeant to frighten him.

Subsequently, he was sent to some base camp for further training. It is well known in any war that the most charming characters are not found at base camps. There is something about the atmosphere of base camps, or at least there was in World War I, which encouraged an excess of spit-and-polish. It also encouraged an excess of petty, senseless, oppression. The kind of thing which my father had no use for.

In his base camp my father found mugwumps. And the king of his mugwumps was subsequently a very famous Hollywood actor, the late Edmund Gwenn. To say that my father did not like Edmund Gwenn would be the understatement of the century.

After his training, my father went to the front. It was the front of 1916 and 1917, grimly determined to carry on. Possibly it suited my father. He was not letting that kind of thing get him down. He never complained in his letters to my mother.

But even in his mess, my father found the kind of people he had no use for. This was not surprising. The mess was full of what used to be called "temporary gentlemen." Men of ordinary origins, pretending to have stately home backgrounds, or hinting at old mansions surrounded by rolling parkland. Men who liked to give the impression that they had been born on a horse. My father had no use for them. He was confident of his own intelligence and place in the world. He did not have to pretend.

"I told them I'd never ridden a horse in my life before. They didn't like it," he would say afterwards.

He seemed surprised that they didn't like it. It never occurred to him that the puncturing of false pretensions is painful to the ego. But then my father couldn't understand what they wanted with pretensions in the first place.

I'm not sure, of course, that my father did not derive a little quiet satisfaction from the fact that he rode much better than most of them.

As it happened, the Colonel was the only man in the regiment for whom my father had not the profoundest contempt. He was a tough South African and a magnificent man on a horse. The Colonel took my father everywhere with him. He became his right-hand man. The sobriquet of "the Colonel's blue-eyed boy" did not worry my father. The Colonel did not pretend, and neither did my father. They had that in common.

The Colonel's standards were high. Even if the mud was deep, he did not expect to see any on his officers' boots. My father arranged for his batman to meet him and clean his boots and brush his uniform while he remained mounted. He would then ride up, shining and spotless, just as the Colonel expected. My father regarded this attitude, not as a sign of oppression, but as an indication that the Colonel knew what he wanted. He also saw that he got it. It was a point of view which one man of character expected from another.

Armies with horses need fodder. And fodder means negotiations with the local population. It was here that the Colonel's blue-eyed boy with his foreign background came in useful. The fact that he spoke perfect French at a time when it was a rare accomplishment was an asset to the regiment.

To say that the Belgians and the northern French have a regard for money would be an understatement. Every franc is part of their blood and guts. The removal of even a few centimes hurts like a major operation.

It was my father's job to negotiate with the peasants and farmers, and avoid letting them cheat him. The art of achieving this without the sacrifice of the regiment's money or the peasants' pride was an arduous balancing feat. Ambassadors trained for years would find it difficult. It is concerned with human dignity, the natural cupidity of the small farmer, and the secondary necessity of not mentioning money until the amenities had been preserved.

My father enjoyed it. It was like a chess game. The moves were set, but the result was not assured.

"You went into the farmhouse kitchen," said my father. "You didn't give the idea you had come to buy anything. The general impression was that it was a purely social visit."

The peasants would then ply my father with raw brandy. He was an abstemious man. If the peasants counted on the softening-up effect of three or four *petits verres,* then they had the wrong man. He only had two. After that he got down to the crunch. And the crunch was hay.

THE MAPS

"I would mention a price," said my father. "They would look at me reproachfully. Tears would come into their eyes. I would touch upon their love for *la patrie* and *la terre.*"

My father looked at me humorously.

"Of course, we knew before we started, more or less, the price I was prepared to pay, and the price they were prepared to accept. But it was a pity to spoil the fun.

"They would mention another price. I would say the Army weren't millionaires. They would be insulted. I would then compliment them on their courage in the face of bombardment. This would reduce the price a little. They would then compliment me on my French, which raised it again."

"Didn't all this take a long time?"

"Of course."

The 1914–1918 war was not a war of movement. They had time to negotiate.

"Finally," said my father, "I would treat them to a peroration on their courage, devotion to duty, and love of their homeland. They would agree with this. I would mention another price— between mine and theirs. Eventually they would agree, with tears in their eyes, adding, of course, that the British Army were robbing them and their children. And then the bargain would be sealed with half a glass of brandy. There was no point in wasting a whole glass once the deal was through."

When my father rode out on his foraging expeditions, he made his way across country with the aid of large-scale maps. He was good at map reading and enjoyed it.

My father was a very good Catholic. But his particular hate during his Army career was Belgian priests. He always seemed to have trouble with priests. I am not sure now that the trouble was always started by the priests. My father enjoyed a good fight, especially when he was in the right. Naturally, he always was, in his view. He had a fund of stories to prove it.

Apart from fodder, the other great necessity of a horse-drawn army was water. This was where my father's trouble with priests started.

Villagers don't like armies. They overrun the country, they eat everything in sight, they run the wells dry, they debauch the girls, and they disrupt. If they are enemy armies, they sack, pillage, and rape; if they are friendly armies, they requisition, but it comes to the same thing in the end.

During some "push," either forwards or backwards, because the 1914 war usually didn't move very far either way, the regiment rode into a small village.

A sergeant came up to my father.

"They've locked up the wells, sir, we can't water the horses."

"Who have locked them up?"

"The villagers, sir. Can't get no sense out of them."

Considering that the sergeant didn't speak a word of French, except a strange lingua franca which had grown up over the years between the Army and the inhabitants of Flanders, this was not surprising.

My father dismounted, and went down the cobbled street. He approached a group of people. One old woman constituted herself spokesman. She addressed my father in the strange language which the troops and peasants had evolved. I don't remember much of what my father told me about this language, except that the word for child was "picaninny."

My father listened to the woman with impatience.

"If you will speak French, madame," he said, "I could under-

42

stand you. If you could speak English, I could understand you. This language is beyond me."

The woman looked annoyed, and then continued in her guttural Flanders French.

"The wells are locked. We can do nothing," she muttered.

"Who has the key?"

"I don't know, monsieur."

"Yes, you do."

Intimidated by his manner, the woman said: "The priest has taken the key, monsieur."

"Where's his house?"

The woman pointed down the street towards a house on the other side of the church.

Having gained his point, my father calmed down. He thanked her profusely for being so helpful, bowing politely. He was not half French for nothing.

When he had arrived at the priest's house, my father knocked loudly on the door. Nothing happened.

The priest had seen him coming. He did not like officers. Particularly, he did not like English officers. My father continued to knock. Presently a lower window opened, and the housekeeper put her face out.

"The priest is out," she shouted. "He can see nobody."

"That means he's in. Tell him I'm here, and if he doesn't produce the keys, I'm going to get my men to shoot the locks off the wells."

This last sentence he repeated loudly. The threat had an immediate response. The faded shutters on the first floor were flung open. A clerical head appeared.

"You English with your gross manners!" yelled the priest.

"You come here, upsetting the village, and destroying our girls!"

"If you are a priest," said my father, "I am ashamed that I am a Catholic!"

The priest looked astonished. An English officer who spoke perfect idiomatic French, and in addition claimed to be a Catholic, pulled him up short.

"You're not a Catholic!" bellowed my father, seizing his advantage. "You're not even a Christian! You haven't even begun! Whited sepulcher!"

The sound of the keys was heard falling on the cobbled street. The clerical head disappeared. My father picked up the keys and set off to get the wells opened. He handed the keys to the sergeant.

"That was quick work, sir," said the sergeant.

"I just reminded him of his Christian duty," my father said mildly.

"I 'eard you, sir, you was speaking a little loud."

My father was a straightforward man. He found it impossible to understand the attraction of flowery sentiments and high-sounding words without following them up with equivalent actions. He understood that priests were only men after all, but he felt that they ought to be making more of an effort. Their target was to become saints. He hated failures.

Sometimes when I remember the tales my father told me of the 1914 war, it seems as though we are becoming an overnice generation. "Conchies," or pacifists, were despised. But they were not left at home to do light jobs, or be tended by psychiatrists.

"We put them to work on the roads," said my father. "As fast as the roads were shelled the conchies had to mend them."

Logical, really, for if a man said he did not want to kill, that did not include being killed, or mending roads under shellfire.

The R. A. S. C. was with the Eighth Division. They went into the Second Battle of the Somme with 15,000 men and came out with 1,500. The generals were determined to win at all costs. But my father said that after the Battle of the Somme the troops never again sang on the march.

About the same time, my father had a fine old row with the madame of a brothel. Whether this was included in his then duties of rounding up stragglers, I don't know. She alleged that he was spoiling her business, which, between battles, was in a highly flourishing state.

The argument ended with her slamming the door on his booted leg. He alleged that he was going out. His descendants wonder.

My father once told me a Maugham-ish story of a tart with a large, badly painted Madonna placed directly over her bed. He thought it was very amusing. His story then was that he was investigating her relations with one of his men.

In 1918 my father came home on leave. From Paris he brought a whole outfit for my mother. Shoes, stockings, and a wonderful lace dress with petticoats to go underneath it.

"I would go into the shop," said my father, "and pick out a girl of the shape and coloring of your mother."

He must have enjoyed that bit.

"I would get her to try on all the clothes, petticoats and all, and pick the things I liked best."

Men shopping for their women had a lot of fun in 1918. And Frenchwomen like to please.

My father liked my mother to look chic. He was particularly

proud of her tiny feet, and felt that it was only in Paris that he could find the exact foil to their attractions—beautifully cut patent shoes with gray suede uppers. When I see these period pieces in old books of costume, it seems odd to think that these were the clothes which my father chose with such care in the Paris of long ago.

My father was not demobilized until the end of 1919. No one was in a hurry to have thousands of men thrown upon a country which had no jobs for them.

The Colonel put my father in charge of a concert party. The fact that he knew nothing about show-biz did not deter my father. The nearest he had ever got to show-biz was playing the violin rather badly. But a concert party was no problem to a man with organizing ability and self-confidence.

My father recruited all the actors he could find, including three female-impersonators, and paid a visit to Paris for materials to dress them in.

"The men were in a mood to mutiny," he would say afterwards. "I didn't blame them. They'd done their job. They wanted to go home."

Flanders is a hostile country. When the wind blows over the flats it hits you in the face like a whiplash. No wonder the men wanted to go home.

"I became very important with my concert party," said my father, with his usual modesty. "We had to keep the troops amused. Besides, the actors were only too pleased to get their hand in again. Of course, I was able to help out with my fiddle," he would add.

The expression on my mother's face mirrored pain at the

thought of my father's capacity as a musician. But she was restrained. She let her eyes say everything. That was quite enough.

In 1919, my father came home to a grateful country. His firm had cheated him of £3,000 in commission which they owed him, and had given his job to a gentleman who had judged his services to be more valuable on the home front than in the cold and damp of Flanders. His directors were kind when they explained about the less well paid job they had allotted my father.

"They had the grace to look sheepish," said my father. I was not surprised. My father did not suffer fools or crooks gladly or in silence.

He went off and bought himself a large steak and a pint of beer and reflected on his future. His luncheon finished, he walked down Piccadilly. On the corner of St. James's Street he caught sight of a face and figure he remembered.

It was Edmund Gwenn.

He was standing complacently on the corner of St. James's waiting for the traffic to stop.

My father was not in a good mood. Mr. Gwenn seemed to him at this moment to symbolize the whole damned setup—base camps, home front, and all.

"I stood there on the corner of the street," said my father, "and thought a damned great black eye would do him good. I stood there, weighing up the pros and cons of hitting him. While I was thinking it out, the traffic started again, and he crossed the road. He still looked complacent. He didn't know what he had missed."

47

My father looked reflective, but still a little regretful. "I have often wondered," he said, "what would have happened if I had hit him."

His maps are thick, linen-backed, and in much better condition than many road maps which have since been used in the fifties, or even the sixties. The scale is 1 inch to 1.58 miles, so they don't show great stretches of country. One shows the country around Tournai, and the other around Amiens.

They were used by my father as he rode around in the mud. I have them in my desk drawer.

Valueless, of course.

6 ✤✤✤

The Statue

ALTHOUGH troublesome priests were a phenomenon which cropped up from time to time in my father's life, priest-ridden was not a word which could be applied to him. His mother may have been an overpious convert, but from his father he inherited a strong streak of French skepticism. It was not that he was in the least anticlerical. He was quite willing to help out in the Church when needed. But he was not inclined to take the sermon for the deed. Probably this was one reason why he never became one of those people who are so disillusioned by the conduct of their soul-healers that they give up religion.

My father had absolutely no intention of letting any priest drive him into disbelieving in God. God was just as much his affair as any priest's.

The writer who said that the fact that an author slept with his cook was nothing against his prose, exactly expressed my father's attitude towards the priesthood.

He was apt to say that he knew holy priests who preached

very bad sermons, and worldly priests who could worst him in a religious argument. His favorite story about an eminent bishop was that he had been described as "all bleeding heart and no bloody head."

One could, in fact, say that he took his priests with a pinch of salt. He gave them the benefit of the doubt. There was no sense in pushing one's chances too far. After all, they were only men. And damned annoying ones sometimes.

In the twenties my father paid two long visits to America. He loved it. He enjoyed the Americans' zest for business and their easy manners. He was not struck with the depth of their culture, and found their food quite tasteless, but then you can't have everything.

The thing he really didn't like, both in Britain and America, was the preponderance of Irish priests. He was not very fond of Irish priests. For one thing, there were too many of them, and for another, he had a poor view of their attitude to religion. They took too much on themselves, like being right all the time, which he knew they weren't. It was clear to him that *he* was always right. There was an arrogance about their attitude towards religion which really annoyed him. Also they were narrow-minded. He liked religion to have a bit of a two-way stretch. Incense was for burning in church, not at home in the drawing room. Once their albs were off, then, by heaven, priests were no whiter than he was, unless they had proved it to his satisfaction.

My father's rumbling discontent with Irish priests came to a climax when he went to America. It was difficult to get away from them, they seemed to be everywhere. Also, according to my father, their brains were not of the keenest caliber. The unfortunate part of it was that it was difficult to avoid going to confession to them.

Going to confession was rather a performance as far as my father was concerned. He always looked a bit portentous about it. When I was a small child, it occasionally crossed my mind that he had some terrible sins to confess. Later, I wondered whether he was assaulted by what, in our world of Popery, are called "scruples." "Scruples," according to the book, consist in having large doubts about small matters. Confessionals are often haunted by old ladies boring priests stiff with "doubts and scruples."

But I decided in the end that my father was not troubled either by deeply dyed black sins, or by doubts. He was simply not sure whether he agreed with the priest to whom he went to confession. He was just weighing the priest up and seeing if he came out on the right side of the balance sheet.

In the U. S. A. he once went to confession in a large city. It may have been New York, Chicago, or Boston—I can no longer remember.

He said his prayers, and entered the confessional.

"Bless me, Father, for I have sinned."

An Irish voice replied. My father recounted his sins. In mid-narrative the Irish voice interrupted him. It asked him a question. What the question was I don't know. However, my father regarded it as impertinent.

"If I had," said my father angrily, "I would have said so."

The Irish voice replied equally angrily. From the pious murmurs of the church a dispute rose up. The waiting penitents looked around in amazement. Their old mothers had often told them that no one argued with the priest. His word was law.

Whatever he said you accepted.

Further exchanges took places. The priest was really rattled. No one answered him back in the confessional; it was unheard of both in Erin's green isle and in the larger spaces of the American continent. Penitents never replied. It was an axiom laid down. A further angry response from my father finally provoked the priest beyond endurance.

"I refuse you absolution, solemnly and finally," said the priest. "We'll see about that!"

My father got up and angrily crossed the church. He walked down the line of confessional boxes until he found one which had a name which did not smack of Erin. He knelt down.

"Bless me, Father, for I have sinned. That fool over there has refused me absolution!" he snorted.

He pointed across the church. Whether the priest without the Irish name was intimidated by my father, or whether he had had trouble with the Irish himself, family history does not recall. The priest managed to calm my father down. He pointed out the value of acceptance of the irritating habits of others, that one should offer up these little setbacks as part of the spiritually educating process of living.

"You mean you should suffer fools gladly?" asked my father.

The priest nodded gently.

My father was willing to accept the fact that the Irish priest was a fool. He felt that it was a mitigation of his offense in not giving him absolution. After a short soothing talk, the non-Irish priest got my father in a better frame of mind. The penitent calmed down. He received his penitence with a feeling compounded of humility and a certain satisfaction that the Irishman hadn't got away with it. Holy Mother Church is tolerant. Stormy penitents need to be placated.

When I was a child my father was actually friendly with one Irish priest. He was an extremely handsome man. He had the kind of looks which Shakespeare describes as "black." Dark, springing hair, deeply set eyes, and a very intelligent expression. He often used to come round for an evening and then would argue philosophy, apologetics, and doctrine with my father. They both enjoyed a good set-to. Sometimes my father would argue in favor of paganism, just to give his mind a larger view of the truth.

My mother thought the priest was narrow-minded. He did not take a good enough view of women. He had a slightly St. Paul view of women which annoyed her.

"It's all very well for him to advocate women having a child every year," she would say. "He doesn't have to have them."

The priest was the intelligent eldest son of a peasant family. Unfortunately, he became an alcoholic. They did what they could for him, his superiors in the church, but in the end they failed.

"It was a pity he had to die like that," said my father, "but it's easier to come from halfway up than from the bottom."

The priest had been taken up by some very rich people who had spoiled him. Perhaps he did not have a true vocation. It's a sad lonely life being a parish priest, not inspiring like being a monk where the order and beauty of a community life can support the weaker vessels. Being a priest is a career in Ireland. In this case, it was a career which ended badly.

My father gave parish sermons very short shrift. When we lived in the country, and he sang in the choir, it was very simple for him. He just went down the choir steps and out into the garden of the church and smoked a cigarette.

"I have it nicely calculated," he said to me. "The parish priest gives a sermon which lasts just the length of a cigarette. Usually by the time I have put it out, it's time to get up into the choir again for the Creed."

Pa's singing in the choir was not as popular as it might have been with the rest of the family. It meant we all had to be on time, and it didn't improve his temper. Rounding up four children, a wife who is continually going back for things, a recently converted nanny, and a maid, is not a task for a man of short temper on a Sunday morning. He usually got the car out and parked it in the lane outside the gate. He then, on one typical occasion, adopted the simple direct method. He sat there with his hand on the horn. The noise was deafening. It was punctuated with shouts of distress, anger, and fury, directed by the rest of the family against each other and against the author of the noise. Feet pounded up and down the stairs. Cries of agony arose about lost missals, rosaries, gloves, and money. The grandfather clock in the hall struck the fatal hour of eleven. Outside in the lane, under the summer green of the trees, the noise continued.

It had the required effect. Everyone piled into the car. It shot off down the lane. Judith fell off the back seat. Nanny furiously put her hat straight.

Silence ensued.

"I've come without my prayer wheel," said Mark.

My father, by this time in a white-hot rage, and feeling rather religious, replied coldly.

"That is not the way to talk about your missal!"

THE STATUE

"Don't annoy him," said my mother. She secretly enjoyed his rages. They were exciting. They exuded a sense of power. There was something about them which had the same effect as the entrance of the bull at the *corrida*. This was the way men should behave.

We drew up outside the church with a scream of brakes. My father disappeared into the choir with my sister Suzanne.

She was the only one who had inherited the Collins musical ear. She had a high, clear, sweet voice, like a boy's. The rest of us had a hard job to pound out even a rousing old favorite like "God Bless the Pope."

No one can say that holy Romans have the best hymns. A good many of them were written by a cleric called, rather improbably, Father Faber, and, honestly, not even a devoted Roman can say he was inspired. He seems to have worked closely with his rhyming dictionary. Fortunately the Mass is sung in Latin and *dominus vobiscum* is Faber-free. Even my father's voice sounded quite good, singing in Latin, cushioned by a chorus of sopranos. I don't expect my grandfather would have thought so. He could spot a wrong note a mile off. But he was a Protestant, and hadn't been in a church since his son died in 1875.

It worried me a bit, when I was small, that my grandfather didn't go to church. But no one else in the family seemed concerned about it. No one tried to convert him. I once asked my father about my grandfather. My father said that he was a good straight man, and that was really all that mattered. Perhaps he thought my grandfather, that tough old military Victorian, was not good conversion material. There's no sense in running deliberately into a barrage.

CHEAPEST IN THE END

By and large, my father didn't hang around the Church. He did what he thought was needed and that was that. It was possible that he thought that if he got too close he might get into an argument. He was full of ideas, some of them of an unconventional nature, and Holy Mother Church likes to move slowly. When I was at school, he tried out a few of his ideas on the nuns, with a marked lack of effect.

I loathed the convent I went to. It was run by a Belgian headmistress. I am quite sure her methods would have been admirably suited to a school off the Avenue Louise. But they didn't suit England, and more particularly they didn't suit me. Once I had got beyond the stage of being capable of being oppressed, I became tiresome. The headmistress complained about me to my father.

"She's a bit of a rebel," he said tolerantly. "I don't know why you don't make her a prefect. That would settle her."

The Belgian nun looked shocked. Her starched veil seemed to become even stiffer. She fingered her ebony cross.

"Always make the leader of the revolutionary movement prime minister," he added.

The nun did not reply. This English sentiment did not appeal to her. She continued to suppress me. I continued to persecute her. Rules led to more rules, and I was antirule. My father didn't reproach me. He said she was handling me wrong, and was quite tolerant about it. He continued to be tolerant until she handled him wrong. She kept him waiting in the drive for nearly an hour on a cold spring afternoon, because she had changed the rules about Sunday outings.

I was then sixteen, and leaving school. My father's reply to the new rule was quite short and sharp. He took my sister

56

THE STATUE

Suzanne away as well. Nuns had to be kept in their place.

When you are young you take an atmosphere of good sense and tolerance for granted. It seems as natural as the air you breathe. Later on, when you realize that people lie, cheat, drink, and whore, and yet are amusing and even pleasant, you become worldly-wise. The simple-minded ideas of your childhood seem old-fashioned, slightly jejune. The idea that doing wrong would be punished tends to become so ridiculous as to be laughable. Really! All around one saw people who were enjoying themselves, and with no reference to the ideas of the Ten Commandments.

When my father was middle-aged he said to me, with a slightly rueful smile, "The older I grow the more I realize that one really does have to become like a little child."

My father's sentiments often embarrassed me. Youth likes to laugh, usually *at* things, not *with* them. I was embarrassed. I said nothing.

Now that I am middle-aged, I am not sure that retribution doesn't catch up on people. But not in a simple way.

Hazlitt says that a man's look is the work of years, for it shows his habit of mind. It shows how he has lived, and gives you a neat insight into his pet vices. Everyone over forty-five has made his own face. And a very grisly retribution it sometimes is. It is not that people lose their hair, go gray, or get potbellies. Some quite pleasant-looking people are bald, with potbellies.

It's much subtler than that. Slack mouths which indicate too many women enjoyed, eyes which congeal over the idea of money, hands which twitch for a cigarette, or tremble when they fill a glass, an expression of self-contempt or anger at the success of others.

I'm not very fond of looking in the glass. It's like Dorian Gray's portrait. You never quite know what you are going to find there in the morning.

My father believed that men who cheated and deceived their wives were punished. I believe they are punishing their own faces. It's the same idea.

But although my father's ideas may have been philosophically simple, they often in reality led to stormy incidents.

Because he was a Catholic, he was not allowed to belong to the Freemasons. The hierarchy still believes that Masons are given to dark deeds against church and state. The fact that they are, in England, a collection of middle-aged businessmen trotting around muttering about the Great Architect of the Universe and clad in blue and white aprons, and overeating at the Café Royal, doesn't seem to have occurred to anyone. The Church is not really "with it" about English Masons. So my father joined a sort of mild Catholic version of the Masons, called the Catenians.

Some Catholic friends got him to join. They gave my father the impression that there were a lot of "jolly good chaps" in the Catenians.

As I remember my father's friends from my childhood, they all seemed to be genial men, exuding the smell of cigar smoke and happiness. They were pleased with themselves and their achievements. Most of them had made their own way up. They were not concerned with social climbing, or with envying people in other spheres than their own. They had nice houses, families growing up, and they were satisfied.

The "jolly good chaps" in the Catenians recommended by my father's friends proved illusory. At least to my father. They were the usual set of fools. My father had a positive genius for unearthing fools. For some reason they had voted themselves into some sort of office. My father thought this was a mistake, especially as they made very bad speeches. So he "had a go at them," as he described it. He was always "having a go" at people. He made barbed speeches against them. He enjoyed it. He polished every phrase.

His dream when he was young was to be a barrister, and he exercised his stifled rhetorical gifts on them. The climax came when he described them as a "permanent line of pompous pontiffs." He was rather pleased with the phrase. They weren't. They never forgave the word "pompous." They voted themselves into office again, and my father resigned.

He transferred his affection to politics. He had always been interested in politics, and he belonged to the National Liberal Club. This was rather unfortunate, as in those days it was simply stuffed with Nonconformists and lower churchmen. But it gave my father a good chance to "have a go at them."

He unearthed a good clutch of dolts and fools in the National Liberal Club. They were also teetotalers, Sunday kill-joys, and "damned narrow-minded." He taunted them with the fact that the first miracle in the New Testament was the turning of water into wine. He followed it up with references to the ass falling down the well on the Sabbath. He had a thoroughly good time. He never resigned from the Club; he had far too much fun there. Although, even he admitted that in those days the decorations were deplorable and the food much worse.

The real thing which attached him to the National Liberal Club was the fact that he had great clutches of people with whom he could disagree and provoke into argument. It would have been a pity to pass up such a unique opportunity for dispute.

The only man my father had any use for at the National Liberal Club was John Burns. He had a great admiration for him. Once when I was lunching there I was introduced to him. I didn't realize then that John Burns was a part of a marvelous past, along with Bernard Shaw and all the pioneers of that age. He just looked rather a nice old man to me.

"There goes a really great figure," said my father. "And he's shrewd, too. I once used the phrase 'a disinterested politician' to John Burns, and he looked at me and smiled. 'I have been in politics all my life,' he said, 'and I have yet to meet a disinterested politician.'"

There was a time when my father was offered a safe Catholic Liberal seat in the East End. But his directors wouldn't let him put up for Parliament. They thought it would take up too much of his time, and they were quite right.

With the decline in Liberalism, he lost some of his political fervor and voted Conservative. Just about the same time he took up organizing funds for some Church charity. I have forgotten what its name was. It was always known in the family as "Pa's society for saving seamen from tarts." We thought it a tough nut to crack, though we were quite prepared to go to the ball Pa organized at the Dorchester, which was the climax of his efforts. It also proved to be the end of his exertions for organized charity.

He had discovered that charitable institutions were also stuffed with "fools and dolts." But before he left, Pa had had a couple of good rows with a monsignor whom he took a poor view of. He thought the Bishop ought to get rid of him.

THE STATUE

"The less I see of the hierarchy, the more religious I become," he said furiously.

I've still got the statue of the Sacred Heart which we bought at one of the charity "do's." My father bought two. He had his own gilded. Being a poor specimen of religious art, it needed something done to it. Mine is still bronze, and it's lost its halo. I suppose that applied to most of us.

7 ❦ ❦ ❦

The Mahogany Chair

TOLSTOY says that all happy families resemble each other. I don't think this is true. Unhappy families have a ghastly monotony of distress and disappointment which colors the current literary scene with a general mid-gray.

Happy families are places where the most fantastic quirks and peculiarities are taken for granted, where large plants and small can flourish in the same seedbed.

When I was a child I took it for granted that everyone's grandfather played the clarinet so that his grandchildren could dance a gay jig or polka. This was the kind of thing which grandfathers were expected to do regularly. My grandfather was a beautiful musician and played his instrument with the greatest delicacy, even in old age, in spite of his rheumaticky fingers.

We children would dance round the nursery in the greatest excitement. But it was an excitement tinged with fear. Suddenly, he would blow a low sinister note in the middle of a jig, which would frighten us into rushing under the table.

THE MAHOGANY CHAIR

I have no doubt that modern psychologists would object to this sudden change from the gay to the sinister. It would injure the budding security-feeling of the child. But you could also say it gave us an insight into the sudden change from the cheerful to the weird, and was a valuable preparation for life.

Although my mother had never played the piano professionally, her father had treated her like a professional. Bad technique was not to be tolerated. The result was that she played extremely well, with a sure, definite touch in keeping with her character.

I can remember how, as a child, the sound of Chopin echoed through the house on a spring morning. But Chopin played as a professional would play it. No tinkling amateur-status drawing-room Chopin. I took it for granted that everyone's mother played Chopin before lunch. I also imagined that everyone's mother played Chopin well.

My grandfather played the violin as well as the clarinet, and during my mother's engagement he made a grave mistake. He had taught my father the violin.

Those were the days of the musical evening, and my mother, no doubt in the first flush of her love and admiration, fancied that a duet consisting of my father playing the violin, accompanied by herself on the piano, would have a certain charm.

She had forgotten one thing. My father, although full of spirit and determination, had no ear for music whatever. She and my grandfather, like all professionals, had the heartiest contempt for the amateur. And there was no doubt that my father was a real amateur. He learned how to play. He learned the tunes, he learned enough to give himself a good deal of fun. But he hadn't a chance.

CHEAPEST IN THE END

It isn't fair to mix amateurs with professionals. Instead of the charming duet which my mother had fondly imagined, the set-up became a trio. Two professionals and an amateur.

Because of my father, their repertoire was scaled down. It became Gilbert and Sullivan, Gounod's *Ave Maria,* and some of Schubert's simpler works. This alone was enough to exasperate my grandfather. "Damned drawing-room muck," he called it.

When they practised before their musical evenings, or even during them, my grandfather would rap out the time with his foot, military style, and my mother would raise her eyes to heaven and give silent groans at my father's lack of tone or wrong notes. The piano accompaniment was spirited and well done, the clarinet's sweet professional tones rang out, and then, plodding along behind came the violin, the hopeful amateur, like a cheerful mongrel which has strayed into a pedigree dog show.

"Always a bar behind!" my grandfather would mutter, furiously stumping off before the polite applause of the visitors had ceased.

Sometimes, of course, the quarrels stopped the show. One visitor was heard to remark that he enjoyed the quarrels more than the music.

I used to be brought down to say good evening to the visitors, and sometimes I was allowed to stay up while the family trio played. I sat bolt upright, wearing a fluffy dress and a taffeta bow. I didn't stay awake, of course. I developed quite a technique of sleeping sitting up. The chair I sat in is in the drawing room now. It used to have a cover of Chinese silk with pagodas, but now it's covered in velvet.

But neither quarrels, nor rude remarks, nor lack of skill

deterred my father. He used to practise regularly on his violin. If British grit could do it, then he was a violinist.

One day I came into the hall. My grandfather was standing there listening. The sunlight lit up his granite face. His expression showed acute distress.

"Is anything the matter, Grandpa?" I asked.

"Listen!" he said in dramatic tones, pointing towards the drawing-room door. "Just listen!"

I heard my father's violin.

"Don't you like him practising?" I asked.

"I'd rather have my behind rubbed with a brick," said my grandfather. "Why does he always play the bit he knows? Why doesn't he play the bit he doesn't know?"

My grandfather, although musically gifted, had no great insight. To practise the bit you don't know is to be a professional. The hopeful amateur, on the other hand, is so happy to hear a tune, any tune, coming out of a conglomeration of strings and wood, that he likes to hear it again and again. There he is —actually playing! Marvelous, how does he do it? Why bother one's head with bits which don't come out right? That way lies depression and discouragement. On with the dance and "Take a pair of sparkling eyes."

My mother had a contempt equal to my grandfather's for my father's gifts as a violinist.

"Well, why did you let him play?" I asked.

"It was better than his singing," she said. "You should have heard it. A kind of falsetto tenor. His mother encouraged him," she added darkly.

When we were young we lived on the outskirts of London, and then, as the family grew we moved to the country. My mother took the opportunity to sell the piano. I think she thought it would finally put the idea of music out of my father's mind.

The house was not even in a village. It was a remote Tudor farmhouse a little prettied up over the years. That would be the end of musical evenings. The violin was put into a top cupboard. Life settled down.

Until one day a tweedy lady called. Later, my mother opened the drawing-room door, and there she was, sitting in animated conversation with my father over a glass of sherry.

"Your husband has very kindly agreed to help us out," said the tweedy lady, gushingly, under the spell of my father's charm.

"Help you out?" said my mother suspiciously.

"So sweet of him. We are all most grateful."

My mother looked at my father. He had on his rather false social smile. She feared the worst.

"What is he going to help you out with?" said my mother, moving with extreme caution.

"Hasn't he told you?"

My father took a gulp of sherry and looked happily out of the window towards the garden.

"No."

The innocent woman galloped on towards Beecher's Brook.

"Our amateur Operatic Society, of course," she said.

My mother's expression congealed into coldness.

"None of us can sing," she said with finality.

"Oh, of course you're not going to sing," laughed the tweedy lady, melodiously. "You're going to help us with the orchestra.

THE MAHOGANY CHAIR

Your husband has been telling me what a wonderful pianist you are, and he is obviously a talented violinist. And I hear your father plays the clarinet. What a nest of talent!"

The rest of the conversation was like a two-sided triangle. My mother contributed little to the general glee and happiness of the lady from the village Operatic Society and her new-found nest of songbirds. After a while even the visitor noticed a certain chill in the atmosphere.

Both my father and my mother walked with her to the door.

"So glad you're going to join us," she said as she got into her small car. "You can't imagine what a relief it is! We can get the singers. It's musicians like yourselves we need so badly."

She drove down the drive and disappeared round a curve in the lane.

My mother turned slowly on my father.

"How did she find out we played?" she asked in a tinny voice.

"I might have mentioned it to a man in the train," said my father nervously.

"You talk too much," said my mother, "especially about music."

"Well, we can't get out of it now," said my father loudly.

He was on the point of getting into one of his rages. The cold shower of my mother's taunts was unpleasant after the warm glow of appreciation.

"I'm not going to try to get out of it," he added.

My mother found herself up against the firm rock of a refusal to budge. She knew the signs. So she shifted her ground.

"We can join if you like—but I'm not going to play the

piano," she said.

"Not going to play the piano? But you can't play anything else."

"I can learn something else," said my mother, in her professional tone.

"Learn another instrument!"

My father was appalled at the idea. He had been scraping away at his violin for twenty years, and even he, optimist though he was, could well see that it hadn't been a complete success. And here was his wife calmly proposing at the age of forty-four to learn another instrument.

"What instrument are you going to play?" he asked, disbelievingly.

"I haven't decided yet," she said, in her sharp voice, the voice she used when things weren't going quite the way she wanted them. "I shall ask my father."

My grandfather had a sitting room on the first floor overlooking the garden. Here he read the papers, listened to the radio, and kept up a good fog compounded of warmth from the coal fire and tobacco smoke. In the summer he sometimes sat in a sheltered part of the garden out of the wind. The rest of the time he walked. He walked immense distances for a man of over eighty—five, six, seven miles in a day, at a steady even pace, taking an interest in the countryside, and especially in the flowers. My mother went into my grandfather's sitting room.

"Clemmy's joined the Operatic Society," she said succinctly, seeing no point in softening the blow.

My grandfather lowered his newspaper.

"Oh, my God!" he said. "He's not going to sing?"

My mother shook her head. "We're all booked to play in the

orchestra."

"I suppose it could be worse, but—" My grandfather sighed. The prospect of my father playing again aged him more than a ten-mile walk.

"I'm not going to play the piano," said my mother, "I've quite made up my mind about that. I thought of learning another instrument."

"Good idea," said my grandfather, casually, as though somebody had suggested switching on the electric fire.

"What do you suggest?"

My grandfather lowered his paper again. "You don't want to do much work?"

"That's the idea."

"Well—there's the piccolo, but it's not as easy as it looks." He glanced at my mother. "You'd like the flute, but you haven't enough wind."

Various other instruments were mooted and rejected. Finally, my grandfather said, "I don't think you could really do better than the double bass."

They were both delighted with this idea. The fact that my mother was only five foot one and a half did not deter them in the least.

"The double bass is one of the most important instruments in the orchestra," said my grandfather, enthusiastically. "It gives the depth, the tone, the darkness to the orchestra. You'll like the double bass."

The next thing to be decided was whom to engage to teach my mother the double bass.

"I went to Brighton last week," said my grandfather. "There's a man in the orchestra there; he hasn't got a bad tone."

"I'll ask him," said my mother.

The following day she drove to Brighton, sent a note around to the double-bass player, and over tea at the Grand Hotel the negotiations were concluded. Mr. Sidney Green agreed to teach my mother the double bass. He was to come twice weekly by train from Brighton—but only on condition that my mother practised. She agreed to do this religiously.

"Otherwise," said Mr. Green, "there would be no point in the lessons. I can't, of course, teach you more than the rudiments. Enough for amateur playing."

"Quite."

"You'll need a double bass. Must start off with your own instrument," said Mr. Green. He scribbled an address near the Charing Cross Road where my mother might be able to purchase an instrument of suitable caliber.

"Tell him I sent you," said Mr. Green darkly. "Don't let him know it's for amateur stuff. You can't be too careful."

The bass fiddle was purchased and the lessons commenced.

Mr. Green was a tall man. He looked more like a prosperous grocer in a small town than a musician. Behind his instrument, however, his thin face took on a purposeful look, his eyes narrowed, and he concentrated on the work in hand. My mother learned quickly. There was only one slight drawback to her prowess as a double-bass player. You couldn't see her at all, because the instrument blotted her out.

Nothing could be perceived except a hand holding a bow and another hand on the strings. It was a little uncanny. Like one of those trick films.

All through the summer the lessons went on. Twice a week in the hot summer days, the thump-thump of the double bass echoed through the house.

My sister Judith was about four at this time, and Nanny seized on the lessons to invent an entirely new punishment:

"If you're not good, you will have to go and sit in the drawing room while Mummy is practising the double bass!"

This threat was enough to keep any child in order. When the summer ended, Mr. Green was satisfied enough with my mother's progress to pronounce her fit to play in an amateur orchestra.

The village Gilbert and Sullivan company, as I remember it, could not have been very good. But the performances gave a lot of pleasure, especially to the performers, and were afterwards written up in laudatory terms in the *Mid-Sussex Times*.

My family were then in great demand for stiffening amateur orchestras all over mid-Sussex. They played in operatic societies, at Hurst College, and in all sorts of concerts, and their departure from the house was always quite a spectacle. It consisted of my father driving his Buick furiously, with my grandfather bouncing up and down on the back seat as the car shot out of the drive, while the rear was brought up by my mother driving a small blue Austin Seven with the double bass sticking up through the sunshine roof.

After the first performance of *Patience* I said to my grandfather: "How did Daddy get on?" An ingenuous question.

My grandfather's face took on a very tormented expression. "Fortunately," he said, "he wasn't the *only* violin. And happily the singers were diabolical, so no one noticed."

My mother very soon got bored with things. After a while her trips around the country with the double bass palled. Now that she could play to her satisfaction, the operation had become tiresome.

"I've decided to give up playing," she said to my father at breakfast one day.

He looked pained. His hand remained poised halfway to his mouth, the toast and marmalade untasted. Giving up music, just when everyone was getting on so well!

"Besides, Grandpa is getting too old to play."

"Nonsense," said my father optimistically. My grandfather was after all only eighty-six.

"His fingers are too clumsy for the clarinet keys," said my mother, who was always prepared to look unpleasant facts in the face.

"What about *The Yeomen of the Guard?*" said my father, with a disappointed face.

"He's decided to conduct," said my mother.

And a very fine job he made of it. I remember his stiff military figure conducting the amateur orchestra with precision, downbeats nicely exaggerated, nasty looks at my father's quavering violin, a look in the direction of his invisible, double-bass-playing daughter, a reproving glance at the pianist.

It was a flourishing, professional, last performance.

The following week my mother announced that she had decided to sell the double bass. It was loaded into the car for the last time. I watched it disappearing round the bend in the lane. Now it had come to the parting, I was sorry to see it go, and Nanny had lost an original punishment.

My father laid his violin sadly aside, too. He knew he would never play with the same abandon again. It seemed the end.

Just before he put it away, the strains of "Take a pair of sparkling eyes," with one or two wrong notes, echoed gaily down the hall. It was the last tune he played on it, the old familiar one, the one he loved best and could play best.

"Listen to it!" said my grandfather, disappearing into the drive with his walking stick.

But while he was out there was a phone call. My father answered it. He sounded very pleased. He was happily agreeing to something. When my grandfather came back at teatime, my father greeted him happily.

"Extraordinary thing," said my father, "they just rang up from the presbytery. Father O'Connor wants me to sing in the choir. I often say, when one door shuts another opens."

My grandfather had a moment of recoil.

"Thank God I'm not a Catholic," he said.

8 ❧ ❧ ❧

The Persian Rug

I WAS fortunate in the people who surrounded me when I was growing up. They had one superb quality in common, an unwillingness to compromise with their consciences. They also had an unwillingness to compromise with each other.

There was my father, who knew his own mind and stuck to it. My mother wasn't giving an inch, either. And there was her father, my Irish grandfather, who also had an iron will.

But then he was born in 1846, into the age of iron. They made quite a trio, my relations, even when they had not their musical instruments with them.

My grandfather's family were all musicians, and came from Ireland about the beginning of the nineteenth century. When he was still a child, his father died.

"Ruined by the Marquess of Donegal," said my grandfather darkly.

"If he hadn't met the Marquess, he would have been alive today," he would mutter angrily to himself, even when he was ninety. I worked it out—his father would have been over a hundred and fifty.

Apparently the Marquess had taken up the gay Mr. Collins, and had promoted him and his orchestra. But the volatile Irish temperament of Mr. Collins, senior, had needed strong drink to keep it humming, and he had sunk to an early grave, leaving his wife in straightened circumstances.

In her bereavement, the widow Collins turned to the most distinguished of my grandfather's relatives, his uncle William. Uncle William was quite a big shot in the Victorian world of music. He composed, he conducted, he started the Royal Engineers Band. Possibly the widow hoped that he would help my grandfather. Like most people who are doing well, he did help, but in a modified way. A way which would not give him too much trouble. It is well known that progress can be impeded by impecunious relatives.

Uncle William recruited my grandfather into the Army, and into his orchestra. Apart from that, he does not seem to have been overconcerned with his nephew's future.

Recently a book was written about the history of the Royal Engineers Band. Uncle William figured very largely in it. My mother was not impressed with the picture of her great-uncle. She knew a thing or two about him. She regarded his picture with coolness.

"What they don't say," she said, "was that he was such an old swine that his orchestra smashed his violin to smithereens."

It has been said that history is bunk. It is also one's relations. It was certainly my grandfather, for he could remember more historical occasions than we were prepared to listen to when we were children.

He had seen the funeral of the Duke of Wellington. He was

present when the last wooden warship was launched—"three tiers of guns, she had"—he had seen one of his uncles come back from the Crimea minus two toes, and had welcomed Queen Alexandra on her arrival in England.

You could say that my grandfather was part of the fabric of history. He was knitted into it intimately. As far as I was concerned he did a great deal too much historical unraveling for my liking. Now I am sorry I didn't listen. Then, as my grandfather talked, you could have stretched out your hand and touched history itself.

The Army of 1860 was tough. Soldiers were scum, and they were treated as the scum they were. Officers, walking along the pavement, would push their men into the gutter. Their sentiments as they pushed them were subtly expressed: "Get off the pathway, you dogs!"

Not surprisingly, my grandfather saw a major shot on parade by one of his own men. That was in 1865. In the same year another officer was shot at Aldershot, and a couple more were potted at Preston.

It flashed through the minds in Whitehall that officers didn't seem to be winning friends and influencing people. They brought in disciplinary reforms. You can't say the Army doesn't get the message.

My grandfather lived in barracks in Chatham, and he used to save up his meager pay to go to Covent Garden to listen to opera. He went up to London on smoky train journeys in third-class carriages, with candle ends to light when the train went through a tunnel, rattling into Dickens' London with the prospect of great music at the end of it.

My grandfather naturally had a great enthusiasm for

THE PERSIAN RUG

Dickens, and as he was fond of telling us, he had heard
Dickens read the Trial Scene from *Pickwick,* the Death of
Little Nell, and the Murder of Nancy. When I heard Mr.
Emlyn Williams giving his readings, I remembered my grand-
father. I wish I had asked him more about Dickens.

Twice a widower, my grandfather had one surviving child,
my mother.

I remember when I was about seventeen, and my grandfather was already in his late eighties, sitting by the fire when
he described to me, with tears in his eyes, his first wife, Polly—
how neat, how thrifty, how charming she had been. Over the
years the picture of the young wife sitting in her chair, sewing
on his buttons, and doing her neat Victorian mending, came
like a sad picture of happiness which was gone.

His second wife had a hard job of it. Playing second fiddle is
not a good role, not even when you are married to a musician.
The living have a hard job keeping up with the dead, particularly the youthful dead, such as the neat and charming Polly.

My mama was a gay, lively child with an amusing view of
life. She was brought up to play the piano, and her father made
her practise for hours every day. She may have been quite a
child prodigy, or possibly her father just treated her as one professional would treat another, and made her get on with the job.

By the time she was seven years old, my mother was playing
at charity concerts with her father, where they appeared on the
program as: "Mr. Collins and his little daughter."

Lottie (aged seven) obliged with "Morgenblätter" by Strauss.
It is a piece which is perhaps not top of the classical pops, but
it is still quite a piece for a child of seven. She must have ac-
quitted herself with her usual dash. Somewhere there used to

be a picture of her at school. Her face is amused and amusing, topped by a large silk bow. Her eyes look shrewdly at life, as they do now.

If my grandfather didn't stand any nonsense from his daughter, she didn't stand any from him. She had none of the docility of his two late wives.

When I was very small I took my grandfather for granted as part of the background of our nursery life. It never occurred to me that everyone didn't have an eighty-year-old grandfather in the nursery. I found him very interesting because he used to take me for country walks. My mother hated walks. But he had the most astonishing capacity for walking, and was an excellent companion for a child. He knew the places where the blackberries grew thickest, and always had his stick ready to pull down the topmost branches where the fattest ones were ripening. He realized the absolute necessity of picking chestnut blossoms in spring, or knocking down the chestnuts in autumn. He had a great love for and knowledge of wildflowers, which he called by all the old-fashioned names.

Even in his nineties my grandfather could do a three-mile walk. He said it kept him moving.

He often used to tell me about the walks he took as a boy. Wonderful walks they were, into the cherry orchards and hop fields of Gillingham. I don't know if anyone has been to Gillingham lately. Its cherry orchards and hop fields have joined the eighteenth-century lavender fields of Mitcham. Now there is nothing but brick as far as the eye can see. But in my mind I feel that the hop fields and the cherry orchards exist somewhere, and that my grandfather is still walking through them.

I don't want to give the impression that my grandfather was

a dear old man. He wasn't. He was a tough old proposition, and as obstinate as an Army mule.

Where my father was menaced by damn fools and dolts, my grandfather was menaced by adverse circumstances. Astonishing things happened to my grandfather. They were never his fault.

He would be standing minding his own business, or reading his newspaper, when suddenly clouds of smoke would appear. They would appear to be coming not from around him, but actually from him.

"Grandpa, you're on fire!"

"Rubbish!"

"You are!"

The next minute warmth, stealing in the direction of his trousers, proved the point. His pipe had burnt itself right through his pocket to fall with a smoldering thud on the floor.

"Blast it, oh, my God!"

His attempts to remedy the initial disaster often burnt holes in the carpet, as the stampings and swearings added to the general incendiary situation.

If my grandfather went to sleep in a deck chair in the garden, the seat would suddenly give way, and he would be picked up from the few spars that remained of it. My mother considered him a deck-chair wrecker. She contended that he threw himself bodily into deck chairs. His own idea was that deck chairs were against him.

"Stuff's got no body in it," he would say, surveying the ruins with contempt.

Winter brought no relief to my grandfather. In winter, armchairs were against him. If he went to sleep in an armchair, that would be found to be on fire. A thin plume of smoke would be seen issuing from the interior. My grandfather could never understand it. Pipe trouble again.

Even toasting his toes in front of a good fire held hazards for my grandfather. He woke up one cold day and could not move his legs at all. He tried several times. No amount of effort on his part could move his legs.

"I'm paralyzed!" he shouted dramatically. He was not altogether surprised, he said later. When you are ninety, some such visitation could be expected.

"Nonsense!" said Nanny.

"I tell you I am!" he said angrily. "I can't move my legs!"

Nanny, who was a girl of sound common sense, suggested he might try taking his feet out of his shoes.

"How can I when I can't move my bloody legs?" said my grandfather irascibly. He had quite decided on an electric wheel-chair by this time.

Nanny managed to get his feet out of his shoes. It turned out that his rubber soles had melted with the heat of the fire and stuck to the carpet. It was quite a job detaching them.

There was some affinity between the element of fire and my grandfather. Perhaps it was some primitive form of fire worship. Perhaps he was subconsciously a pyromaniac. As he was always cold, he was continually "drawing the fire up." This consisted of putting his newspaper in front of the grate, propped up by what he called the "fire irons." The paper always caught fire, of course, and he would snatch the flaming fragments down, and stamp on them, and call out, "Oh, my God! oh, my God!" in tragic tones. Sometimes he singed his trousers legs in the process.

At other times he would lend his handkerchief to various children for mopping up paint water or spilt milk. He would dry it in front of the fire, or on the nursery fireguard. He always burned his handkerchief. There were very few things which my grandfather had not been known to burn in his time.

Apart from burning things, my grandfather had other types of misfortune. He fell over a lot, and usually tore his trousers. If he climbed a stile, he would catch his jacket on a nail. If he cut bread, he always drew blood. On the only occasion when he chopped wood, he took off the tip of his small finger. He was not what you would call handy about the house.

Of course, when he played the clarinet or violin it was a different story. Then his fingers were delicate and light on keys or strings.

He was a wonderful clarinetist, and had known most of the musicians and conductors of his day. He should have had an orchestra of his own, but he lacked confidence in himself. He had no push and too much critical sense.

He wasn't only critical of himself. He had seen Wagner conduct. "Rotten conductor," said my grandfather. "They had to send for Richter."

There weren't, now I come to think of it, a great many characters of whom he did take a good view.

"Actors?" my grandfather would say. "A monkey could do what they do! Monkeys, that's all they are."

"Irving!" he said once. "Never saw anything so boring as 'The Bells.'"

We asked him about Bernhardt. Apart from being a foreigner, which he didn't approve of, he said she pulled too many faces.

CHEAPEST IN THE END

My grandfather was very bad value for practical jokes. As children we were very keen on practical jokes, and we didn't care how much trouble we went to in order to make my grandfather's life a misery. The simpler ones included the usual jug of water balanced over his door, flour on his pillow, honey in his washbasin, a frying pan in his bed, and the machining-up of his pajama legs.

"How did you sleep, Grandpa?" we would ask eagerly.

"Like a top!"

His face would be quite cheerful.

This took the flavor out of the joke. We gave up jokes. There was no point if people didn't actually mind about them.

Occasionally, when my grandfather got really exasperated with us all, he would threaten to join the Chelsea Pensioners. It was always his Parthian shot. Actually, he probably fancied himself dressed up in a scarlet coat, marching to the tune of "Boys of the old Brigade." It also gave him a sense of power, because he knew we wouldn't like him to be seen hamming it up in a scarlet coat, wearing all those long-service medals.

When we were ill my grandfather was very assiduous in bringing up medicines. If the doctor said three times a day, then my grandfather would appear three times "regular as clockwork" as he said. He liked doing us good. The nastier the medicine the better he liked it. If we complained, he would take a good slug himself, and pronounce it delicious. He was a great hand at trying medicines; he would take a good dose of anything which came into the house. It was partly out of curiosity, and partly because he felt that anything which tasted nasty was bound to do you good.

He had been brought up on brimstone and treacle, and nothing since then really appealed to him. Modern medicines were really too weak to give one a real shot in the arm. His capacity for trying medicines was endless. My father alleged that my grandfather had even been known to take what used to be called a "female pill."

Although my father and my grandfather had very little in common, they were agreed on some subjects. One was foreigners.

My father, in spite of his French blood, didn't like the French, and my grandfather, in spite of his Irish blood, had no use for the Irish. They had better not grumble about England in front of my grandfather, or they would be told to "get back to their bloody bogs." As a matter of fact, my grandfather had no use for any sort of foreigner. His idea was that there were the English, and they were all right—you could keep the rest.

Of course, in his day you could hardly admit to being English if you were concerned with music. Henry Wood had to write music under a Russian name before it could be played. And it was the custom to dress perfectly ordinary English musicians in Hungarian and Russian hussar uniforms before they performed the simplest waltz. Possibly this gave my grandfather a prejudice against foreigners. Or perhaps it was just that he didn't like foreigners anyway.

I sometimes think the trouble with modern England is over-veneration of foreigners. Foreigners can't be right all the time. And there are flavors other than garlic. It's all very well to be tolerant, but as my grandfather said, in the words of the old saw, if you bend down in Trafalgar Square anyone will kick your behind for you.

My grandfather's hobby was cricket. Even when he was a

very old man he would go off happily, with a packet of sandwiches, and sit in Hove Cricket Ground watching the game
all day under the boiling sun. No one in the family shared his
hobby. No one went with him. He just plodded off in his solitary fashion, enjoying the game like the connoisseur that he
was. When the game was over he came home.

Sometimes we asked him whether he had enjoyed it. Sometimes we didn't.

My grandfather was a good hand at picking up acquaintances
on his solitary expeditions. He liked to boast of his great age.
To those who lived with him it was no astonishment. We took
it for granted. But to outsiders it was a good talking point.

When my parents moved to London in the late thirties, my
grandfather used to do a short turn in the Park as far as the
Round Pond and back to Sloane Street for lunch.

On these walks he was often picked up by old ladies. I think
they thought he was the kind of wealthy old gentleman who
might keep them in comfort for the rest of their days. But my
grandfather, who was being kept in comfort for the rest of his
days, was evasive. If the old ladies got a little too chatty or
forthcoming, he would change his beat.

"You can't be too careful," he would say to me, looking over
his glasses, aged ninety.

His second wife had died over forty years before. He must
have met a good many designing females in forty years, for he
was a good-looking old man. But ninety was no age to be thinking of marrying again for a third time, he would point out.

The Persian Rug is still on the floor. It's got a burn in it, of
course. It reminds me of my grandfather.

9 ❧❧❧

The Secret Garden

ONE of those experts who now infest most landscapes has stated that *The Secret Garden* is a book for an inhibited town child. It was my favorite book. I wasn't a town child.

Perhaps I was inhibited. No one ever troubled to find out. No one bothered about my psychology when I was a child, and I am not sure that it wasn't the best idea in the end. Sink or swim. It is no good bringing up people to think that life is a self-opening oyster. You just give them a knife and tell them to get on with it.

When my parents married they went to Paris for their honeymoon. This was a dashing thing for a couple of their modest pretensions. Foreigners were really foreigners before World War I. They threw their arms about; they had black imperials and waxed moustaches. Cab drivers were irascible and drove dangerously, music halls were shocking, the food was delicate. And you had wine served free with your meal.

It seems odd when you see those old jerky films with men rushing about like little clockwork dummies, and women

85

holding up their skirts against the mud, to think that these were your parents. These were the happy, go-getting people of the early century, the century which was in its dawn, which believed in eternal progress and prosperity. You turn on the radio, and, like a breath of perfume from some idyllic past, comes the easy, hopeful dance music of yesterday. To these waltzes my parents danced into the responsibilities of marriage.

A year after they married, they had a son, baptized Paul, who died at the age of six months of some obscure disease. The surgeons at that time hadn't invented instruments small enough to operate on such a tiny child.

"I shall always remember your mother throwing his toys into the fire. Her face was quite unmoving. She didn't cry," said my father.

But my father was young, he was handsome, he was vigorous. There would be other children. To cheer her up, he moved into a bigger house. He was getting on in business, and success is like a perfume to some women. My mother liked to watch his slim, silk-hatted figure going off to the City.

My father, who never did things by halves, had two silk hats. One he wore, the other he left at the hatters to be ironed. On the way to the office, he exchanged silk hats, putting the newly ironed one on his head. He was ready for the day's work. He liked to be well turned out. The best was always only just good enough for him.

We were a well spaced out family. Twelve years separated me from my youngest sister. Until I was nearly five I was an only child. Such pictures as survive show me to have a small, solemn, doll-like figure. I am usually dressed in white silk dresses, with large butterfly bows on the top of my head, and gold bracelets on my wrist. I didn't eat jam because I didn't like the feeling on my fingers. I was taken for holidays to Brighton, where we stayed in a hotel, and old ladies remarked on my quiet behavior and good manners. I don't sound to have been much fun.

One can only be thankful that Nature provided other children to my parents' marriage, otherwise Frankenstein would have had a baby sister.

My sister was born at home. I remember very clearly the first time I saw her. It is my earliest memory. I had been sent away to stay with relations, and when I came back to the house my mother carried the baby down, dressed in the long lacy robes of the period.

My father stood proudly at the foot of the stairs. My mother bent down to show me the little wrinkled red face.

"That's the new baby—your sister," said my father, in that soupy encouraging voice, which adults often use to children.

I looked at the baby. My sister! That! I peered at it again. My mother bent lower so that I could have a really good look. My only feelings were of intense dismay.

"Aren't you happy to see your new sister?" said my father.

I was always a truthful child. I cannot say that it paid off, but we are stuck with our virtues as well as our vices. I was truthful mostly because it never occurred to me not to look facts in the face.

I had another look at the current fact before me—my sister. We might as well start as we mean to go on, I thought. No use in dissembling.

"Isn't she sweet?" said my father, tenderly.

"No!"

I spoke out in a firm clear voice. My parents looked dismayed.

CHEAPEST IN THE END

But it was the beginning of family life. The well-behaved child with her white silk frocks was no longer alone.

Those hopeful child psychologists who feel, with Wordsworth, that heaven lies about us in our infancy, have never obviously given a moment's thought to childhood. Not to a real childhood. For children are fiends in human shape. As a bunch we were given to most forms of fiendish behavior. A mixture of Irish and French blood is not a good amalgam if you want a quiet life in the home.

Quarrels and cabals were frequent and noisy. With a widely spaced family the number of permutations and combinations in the shape of quarrels, fights, and general unpleasantness is endless. The two youngest against the two eldest, or again the youngest and the eldest against the two middle ones.

My sister and I fought literally tooth and nail. I cannot remember what we fought about, but we would roll on the floor tearing one another's hair out, and digging our nails into one another. My mother never stopped us. I imagine she figured out that someone would win, and that would be a lesson to somebody in the general unfairness of life.

Then my sister would fight my brother, Mark. She was older and heavier, and she usually won. My brother was spoiled by my father, who refused to beat him, and he never got punished. So my mother figured that a good beating now and again from my sister didn't do him any harm.

Then my brother went to prep school and learned to fight scientifically. He came home and knocked my sister all around the nursery and into the fireplace. My mother watched. She conceded it was a good fight. My sister never fought my brother again. So, in a way, justice was seen to be done.

The baby of the family, Judith, with her golden aureole of curls, looked a real dreamchild. She was always clean, always accompanied by Nanny, and in general gave the impression of a kind of little-girl Fauntleroy. My brother thought she was a bit soppy. His favorite game was to call down the garden in a voice which was a perfect echo, "Ju–dith—Nanny wants you–oo!"

Little Judith would come running up, to find a grinning boy peering through the hedge. Finally, exasperated for the hundredth time, she picked up an edger the gardener had left on the path. She hit out at her tormenter, and cut his eyelid open. She was only four, but she had quite a temper. Fortunately she wasn't very strong, and the cut wasn't deep.

Our games were imaginative, and usually taken from the books we were reading. "Christians to the Lions" was a gentle game consisting of my brother and me throwing my sister off a balcony to the dogs on the lawn. There was only one snag— the dogs once got too excited and bit my sister, who was rushed straight off to the doctor.

My father was not good at punishing any of us as children. He could roar with baffled fury in the middle of the uproar, but the long slow deliberate punishment was not in his repertoire. He left that to my mother.

Mostly we were sent to bed. But even that wasn't always the end of the story. We would ring the bell for more pudding to be sent up for supper.

As a gang we weren't very good material for staying in hotels. So mostly we took furnished houses at the sea. As I remember them, they were furnished with a uniform and Victorian ugliness. Owned by ladies in reduced circumstances, they were furnished for letting, and made small additions to their incomes. The wallpapers were dark brown and often varnished. The prints on the walls either soppy or frightening. Children in floppy hats feeding white ponies over cottage walls abounded. Oleographs of Doré's damned in hell, or black-and-white biblical disasters, were frequent. Whatnots decorated the drawing rooms, and the gardens were full of rank-growing marigolds and perennial marguerites.

My father was the perfect father for a houseful of children. He loved children, and he was particularly good value on a seaside holiday. No question of economizing on donkey rides. He paid for half a dozen in a lordly fashion.

On the shore he would construct marvelous sand castles. None of your ordinary castles with a plain tunnel from one side to the other. His castles were the real thing. They had moats, drawbridges, shells for windows, a seaweed garden, a tower with a specially bought flag floating from its turret top.

Each crenelation was carefully cut with a sharp spade. A spade which had been specially bought for the job. We had been to the ironmongers to buy the spade. It had been tested, discussed, and when it was finally approved as exactly right for the job of sand-castle-constructing, it had been paid for, and taken to the shore. My father always insisted on the right tools for the job and damn the cost, and the job of making a sand castle was not a thing to be embarked on lightly. I knew that. My father knew that. And there it stood, a real work of art. A thing of beauty. It was sad to watch the great gray sea licking round its outer walls, to see the gradual decay of the drawbridge, and to watch the crumbling dissolution of the marvelous turret. The flag would be kept, as a souvenir of the fortress which was gone. A fortress which could be kept in the mind after the sea had claimed its reality.

My mother never had much patience with such pernickety activities. She liked to sit on the shore and watch the sea. If it were a hot day, we children would trot up and down, bringing her buckets of water to cool her hands. She was always much too practical, we thought, anxious to do dull things like getting back to lunch, or seeing that the maid brought tea down to the beach. She never could see the intense sadness of leaving a sand castle before the last sad turret had fallen into the consuming sea. And she wasn't disposed to see the fun of eating bananas and bath buns after swimming. That would "spoil their lunch." This was the whole idea. But my mother couldn't see this.

Storming the stockade was another game we enjoyed one year. This consisted of my sister and me, in the house, behind a stockade of deck chairs, being attacked by my father and brother, who threw lumps of earth from the garden. It was a dry summer and the task wasn't as messy as it sounds. When the final break-through occurred, my sister fought a delaying action, while I rushed to the rescue, trying to hold off the invaders with the garden hose. My father laughed delightedly as he dodged the jets of water.

This game, though undoubtedly giving good value, was stopped by my mother. It was getting too realistic. Besides, she said, remember the dilapidations. Mothers are appallingly practical. They can never see that you can't possibly talk to a beleaguered garrison like that.

Mostly, the houses we rented were on the South coast. But one year we took a house at Whitby. It was a stormy, rainy summer, and the beach lay at the foot of steep cliffs. My brother was only four. He had decided that he didn't like climbing cliffs. It appeared to him tiring. Especially when there were convenient donkeys, supplied for a small sum, to take weary travelers, such as himself, to the top. He had a good idea. He just stood at the bottom and roared his head off until my father paid for a donkey. This, like most simple ideas, was radical. It worked because my father couldn't stand the sight of his weeping son, and my mother couldn't stand the noise. My brother carried out this process every day we stayed in the house, nearly six weeks. Children have more stamina than adults, and they know it.

I seem to remember often being ill as a child. Perhaps this is an illusion. But I do know that if I had the slightest ache I was put to bed. My mother, with her Celtic temperament and her memories of the past, would condemn me to an untimely grave like my lost brother Paul.

My father adopted more practical methods. He told me fairy stories. They were good fairy stories, full of action and peopled with just the kind of characters which children like, both wonderful and frightening. As he spoke, a world of glittering palaces, strange wizards, fearful monsters, and incredibly eccentric old wizards, would arise. His heroes, usually noble, or in temporary quest of nobility, were ingenious as well as handsome. They knew instinctively things which most people might have forgotten. Things like how to kill snakes. You pick them up, hold them firmly by the neck, bite off the head, spit it out, and then peel them down like a banana.

His princesses, less active, usually sat about waiting for things to happen to them, but they were so marvelously dressed while they did it that one forgave them their lack of get-up-and-go.

THE SECRET GARDEN

Apart from keeping the invalid amused with stories, my father also liked to cook delicious meals. The sight of those meals was enough to make anyone feel better. Everything was done on a Lilliputian scale. Tiny pieces of toast thinner than a child's small finger, a little fillet of sole cooked in milk, with a delicate sifting of pepper and salt, and a curl of butter resting on it. Bananas, finely cut up, with brown sugar. Oranges carefully decapitated, the pith cut away, the flesh marvelously sliced and ready to have interesting sugar lumps popped inside.

"You can eat a doll's lunch, surely?" my father would say.

And usually I could. The idea of a doll eating lunch had an immediate appeal.

Of course, there was another thing about his children being ill which worried my father. It was doctors. He usually found them very annoying. They treated him like a fool. He knew he was not a fool. And he was vitally concerned that they should know it, too.

The main thing to do with doctors, according to my father, was to see that they knew their job. This was to get his children better. If they hadn't succeeded after a week or so, he just sent for another one.

During the whole history of our childish ailments he found only one doctor who he felt was up to the job of looking after his children. This doctor was an extremely ugly man, brilliantly clever, and very rude. He was consultant to a London hospital, and badly thought of in the town, mainly because he told the truth. This doctor suited my father down to the ground.

"I don't know what's the matter with her," said the doctor, with no preamble, after examining me on one occasion. My father approved of this confession.

"You can send for a specialist, he won't be cheap; he'll cost you fifty guineas; and he may or may not know more than I do," said the doctor.

My father and the doctor looked at one another. They decided to give it another week, and then spend fifty guineas. I got better. Perhaps I decided that illness was expensive. Or perhaps the germs got frightened.

We were all sent to boarding school at the age of eight. My mother said she couldn't cope with us after that. My father didn't get the worst of us, she said. It was all very well for him, but once we reached the age of eight we got out of hand.

The odd thing was that each one of us was taken for an only child. Perhaps it was because we seemed spoiled. Perhaps because we were individualists. Individualists or not, off we went. And the last thing we saw, as the train left the station, was my mother's happy smile as she waved us goodbye and went off to the cinema.

I longed to have a mother who wiped her eye at the station with a fine cambric handkerchief, as mothers used to do in books.

Once we were at boarding school we were expected to work. If we came out second, my father wanted to know why we weren't first. Explanations of the kind that nearly all the class were three years older than we were, were dismissed as irrelevant. His children were clever, he knew that. He expected them to work. Put the two things together, and, *ergo,* they ought to be first.

You weren't expected to be a failure in my family.

The intensity of our religious training at school, with church twice a day, and a thick dose of doctrine every morning, ought to have made us all into religious maniacs or social misfits. It always does in books. I can't say that we qualified as withered primroses. We were all top in catechism and bottom for conduct. If the nuns dared to complain about us, my father blamed the nuns. He reckoned he paid them to keep us in order. If they couldn't manage it, he could, he would say. Obviously he was paying good money to incompetent women. He usually pointed out that we all worked hard. We did. He saw to that. My father's sensitive fingers running down a report were enough to make any child keep its brain really toned up.

The only one in the family who got away with not working was the baby, Judith. My father had mellowed by the time she went to school. Besides, her nuns belonged to an enclosed order and it's not so easy giving holy women a piece of your mind if you have to peer through a grille to do it. Maybe the idea of grilles was to keep men like my father from upsetting the peaceful calm of convent life.

I've still got a copy of *The Secret Garden*. My sister gave it to me a year or two ago. My original copy was eaten by dogs.

It is a sharp reminder of my childhood. As they say, it was written for a gentle, inhibited, town child. Now I come to think it over, I wonder why I liked it so much, and still do. I don't seem to have had a terribly inhibited childhood.

10 ✢ ✢ ✢

The Sepia Madonna

GOING abroad with a wife, four children, a grandfather of eighty-two, and a nanny is not the sort of holiday anyone in their senses would undertake.

My father was not deterred.

It didn't seem to him important that my grandfather considered all foreigners as no better than Hottentots, that Nanny would be in a permanent state of disapproval over the plumbing, that my mother wouldn't be able to get her daily steaming bath, and that children of three and eight would be much happier sitting on the beach at Bognor.

He had got it into his head that the open road was the thing. His romantic nature saw the straight roads of France stretching out in front of him. Not to mention the little wayside cafés, the accordion music, and the soft voices talking the language of his ancestors.

Whatever the faults of the French race—they are hard, they are selfish, their manners are only a piecrust—one of the most enduring and endearing things about them is their sense of home and family. You see them sitting in the restaurant on Sunday in family parties, and you are appalled by their endurance in the face of such family gatherings. This sense of family my father had in abundance—that sharply defined sense of difference between his own and those who were outside the circle —and no doubt he fancied seeing his family sitting around the restaurant table under the chestnut trees, while he had an interesting chat about the menu with the proprietor.

It all started at breakfast. My father had a letter from my sister's French godmother. She announced that she had recently acquired a little hotel, a real retreat, she said, in Normandy. It had been an old monastery. On a hill, overlooking the sea, not far from a beach. The garden was full of old trees, the soft honey-colored walls were covered with roses the whole summer long.

She didn't suggest that my father come with his family. But she knew my father. He saw it all—the old monastery glowing in the evening sun, the roses tumbling in profusion down the ancient walls, the children happily chatting in two languages.

"The old monks' refectory is now our dining room," she wrote. "We are going to specialize in Norman cooking. As you remember, my grandmother came from a little village near Rouen."

"Just think," said my father, "the real Norman cooking, eh!"

"Did she say how much it's going to be?" asked my mother. Her experience of foreigners was that they were a little too sharp on the cash for her liking. Besides, she knew the lady in question.

"Oh," said my father with happy optimism, "she will make a special price for us. Old friends!"

My mother's face remained impassive.

"Has she sent a photograph of the place?"

My father brushed the idea away with impatience. His imagination had been fired. He saw all his family sitting in the old monks' refectory, their plates piled high with sole Normande, tripe *à la mode de Caen,* and Norman cheese at its peak of perfection.

He wrote off at once, booking rooms for the entire family. It was heigh-ho for the open road. Both for him, and for his entire family.

The next step was to book the car on the boat. In those days there was no car carrier, no drive-on-and-drive-off. The car, secured with chains, was swung high above your head onto the deck of the ship. My father decided it would be a good idea to drive down to Newhaven and have a look at the boat.

I was about sixteen at the time. My head was full of ideas gleaned from Michael Arlen, W. J. Locke, and Phillips Oppenheim. The proper way to travel was in the Golden Arrow. Mysterious and remote, one drifted along the platform at Victoria wearing a green hat and an ermine coat, followed by a lady's maid at a discreet distance carrying a crocodile dressing case with gold fittings. It could possibly be, if one raised heavy-lidded eyes, that one might catch sight of a burning-eyed foreigner who had immediately been struck dumb at one's beauty. But otherwise the journey would be uneventful, because of the terrible sense of futility which was weighing one down.

Imagine being dragged off with a load of children to look at a common little cross-channel boat in Newhaven harbor. I just sat in the back of the car—suffering.

When we got to Newhaven all the children jumped out,

followed by Nanny, and went capering off happily to "see the boat which is going to take us to France."

"Aren't you coming?" asked my father.

"No, thank you," I said. It was useless to explain that one had just arrived (unhappily) to meet one's husband at the George V.

I pulled my puce felt hat down further over my eyes. I was rather keen on that puce hat. It didn't look any too good with my navy-blue school coat. But I had improved that by adding a gray chinchilla rabbit collar.

I sat in the car, aloof and mysterious, peering over my fur collar with a blasé air.

My father gave me a look of disgust, and set off towards the quay with the rest of his more co-operative brood.

When the day came, I did bring myself to get on the boat, though from time to time I tried to give the impression that I was traveling alone. However, the boat seemed to be short on mysterious international spies; odd foreigners with burning eyes were lacking; and there wasn't even an obvious king's messenger. Perhaps they didn't use the Newhaven–Dieppe line. I decided to rejoin my family.

Our first view of "abroad" was not very exciting. The beach, the sky, and the sea were all a uniform gray.

"Can't see the difference between this and the sea off Worthing," said my grandfather.

The car was set down on the quay with a bump. My father got in and pressed the self-starter. But nothing happened. No sound was heard except the gray whistling of the wind over the cobblestones.

Somewhere there is a snapshot of the entire family huddled

on a bench. Nanny's face is pinched and cold under her navy-blue nunlike veil, and the rest of us look very wind-blown.

The stationary aspect of the car maddened my father. But he wasn't letting the matter rest. He had decided it was going to be heigh-ho for the open road and it would be so much the worse for everybody if it wasn't.

Soon the surrounding population found out that they had an unusual breed of Englishman to deal with. *Le sang-froid anglais* was conspicuously in absence. This was a man who was prepared to meet them on their own ground. Did they present excuses, he threw them back with neat retorts. Did they find reasons for the impossibility of getting the car moving, he found even more why they should. If they dramatized their situation, then he could bring tears to their eyes with the tale of his ruined holiday and freezing family. In three hours he was on the road.

It was inevitable that the dreamy old monastery should turn out to be cold, practically unfurnished, and on the top of a perpendicular cliff with a perpendicular view of the sea.

My grandfather took one look at the cliff path and said that it was suitable only for goats. Nanny discovered that the lavatory didn't work. My mother turned on the bath tap, and nothing but cold water and dead spiders came out.

All this wouldn't have mattered to my father, but he discovered that when mentioning that the food was served in the old monks' refectory they had omitted to mention that they were apparently still serving the old monks' food. The fish (we arrived on a Friday) was dubious, and was followed by sour stewed apples. Breakfast consisted of rocklike stale bread which had been prudently kept and rebaked in the oven. This was served with bitter chicory in what my grandfather described as "slop basins."

It did not take my father long to discover a little modern family hotel right on the shore near Deauville. The food was very good because there wasn't an Englishman staying in the place.

"How much?" said my mother, always one to get down to essentials.

My father mentioned exactly the same price as he had been charged for short rations in the monks' refectory.

"I'm not surprised," said my mother. "You can't trust friends."

Even my father's face had a tinge of disillusion. Half Gallic as he was, he had an ambivalent attitude towards France. When he was there he felt English. He was not quite sure that he wasn't always being taken for a ride. In this case he had had his worst fears confirmed.

The moment my father arrived back in England, it was inevitable that he felt French. He would say that Englishmen were dull conversationalists and less quick-witted than the French. This split in ideas he never solved, any more than it has been solved by his descendents who share his blood. My own feeling is that when choosing dinner companions to stimulate and amuse, I would plump for the French every time. But if one were picking a foursome for a fire, a mining disaster, or a short spell in prison, I would chose the English. There are times when a lack of wit and imagination can be a distinct advantage.

However, at the time of the monastery disaster my father felt sufficiently Gallic to present Madame with his excuses, a roll of bank notes, and a bunch of roses before shaking the dust of the romantic old refectory from his family's feet. Face must be preserved. The amenities must be respected. If the proprietress had her dignity of hotel proprietor, my father retained his dignity as guest. He could hardly say that he didn't like the dump. He pleaded the delicate health of his robust father-in-law. The height didn't suit the old man. He suffered from vertigo.

"Ptomaine poisoning," said my grandfather in a loud voice.

My second visit abroad was more to my taste. It was decided that I must learn French. Finishing schools in Paris were written to. But my father didn't like the look of the prospectuses. There were ominous items on them. Things like "five evening dresses."

This led my father to think that I might get the wrong ideas about life, or the amount of money he was prepared to spend to have me taught French. There was nothing doing.

Brussels was eventually decided on, and we set off to inspect a school off the Avenue Louise.

This was more like it. This was the kind of traveling I had imagined for myself. First class, and luxury. We stayed in the best hotel in Brussels, with a bathroom for my parents, and a bathroom for me. Between times, of course, we gave our gracious attention to a few of the local sights, like the battlefield at Waterloo, and some of the galleries of Flemish painting.

I am not overfond of Flemish painting. It seems to consist mostly of dead game and fruit, either by itself or accompanied by appreciative faces round a loaded table.

Occasionally, for added realism, the painter will draw in a

dog relieving itself against the table leg. Bosoms bulge out of bodices, faces are hot and greasy, and the loud raucous laughs seem to echo from the canvases. Flemish painting is not delicate.

We also went to the Musée Wiertz. Here we found happy little canvases concerned with death, famine, and cannibalism. They were painted as propaganda against Napoleon. As an introduction to the art of painting, Flemish art is a little coarse in texture.

From Brussels we traveled by international express to Paris. Lolling back in my first-class dining car, I felt that this was the life. Suddenly I knew it was exciting being sixteen, really abroad, and not followed by a crowd of children. My father gave me a glass of white wine for dinner. This was really living. I have never recaptured the feeling I had for Paris that first time.

I suppose it was a compound of being sixteen, of being abroad, of seeing my father as masterful and commanding in French as he was in English, and of the prospect of finding myself actually staying in the kind of hotel I had read about, a real international luxury hotel. At least I thought it was a luxury hotel until my mother saw her bedroom.

One look at the bedroom told my mother that she wouldn't be able to sleep in it. My mother in those days didn't take the rosiest view of hotels. She was always prepared for the worst, and her family were never surprised to receive postcards from her holiday route saying succinctly, "Arrived yesterday. Hotel filthy, leaving tomorrow."

As soon as my mother had announced that she didn't like the look of her hotel room my father sent for the manager.

The manager entered. He was happy, he was expecting

compliments. He started off by congratulating my father on his excellent French. Before the conversation ended he would have been glad if my father had been less well able to express himself.

The hotel manager pleaded, my father remained indifferent to his explanations. He added a pithy word or two, expressing his great disappointment with the hotel, the manager, the land of his forefathers, Paris, and, of course, his bedroom (coupled with his bathroom).

All this might well have been a silent film. My mother and I could not speak French. But you didn't really need to understand. My father's face told us all we needed to know. Finally, having reduced the hotel manager to a stunned silence, my father announced that he was about to take his daughter to see the Tomb of Napoleon. From the look he gave his hotel room, he indicated to the hotel manager that it didn't look as if it had been touched since the Emperor's death. Finally my father added that when he returned from sightseeing he would expect to find that the hotel manager had remedied his errors of judgement.

At a sign from my father we swept out.

My mother was pleased with this scene.

"You never know what he is going to do next," she said to me with satisfaction.

When we came back from sightseeing, my parents were installed in the bridal suite, and a huge basket of red roses was placed on the writing desk with a card expressing the manager's wishes for a happy stay to Madame. Those were ripe days for guests in hotels.

THE SEPIA MADONNA

When I had been in Brussels for three months, I spoke French fluently. I was pleased with myself. My father wasn't pleased. He said I talked French like a waiter. Daily diction lessons were prescribed. There are disadvantages if you have a father with French blood. When you learn French you have to learn it.

Being in the antique business, my father often went to Paris looking for "French pieces," as he sometimes put it. Not that he ever pretended to know anything about antiques. He did, of course, but he always drew a line between men who were experts and those who were hopeful amateurs. He considered that he was only a dabbler. Antique buyers were experts.

"There are no stupider people than amateurs who think they know," he would say, giving me a shrewd look.

When my father went to Paris with his experts to buy furniture, he was plagued by two things. One was his distrust of French businessmen, and the second was his disgust at being continually taken for a tourist. Accompanied as he always was by English companions, they would be approached by touts selling everything from filthy postcards to introductions to special sessions of *danse de ventre*. Although interested in women in the abstract, and by no means prudish, my father was not interested in the commercialization of nudity. He also objected to being taken for a foreigner, a fool, and a dolt.

The thing which pleased him most about the French was their preservation of human dignity.

"One day," he said, "I was walking along the boulevard with a French businessman. We were enjoying the evening air after a good dinner, watching the people and traffic passing by. A prostitute came up to us. I was at a loss. The Frenchman simply smiled, raised his hat, and said politely, 'Merci, Madame.' The prostitute bowed, smiled, and passed on to other potential customers. No one's feelings were hurt."

My father's voice was full of admiration. This was the way life should be lived, with politeness and with panache.

To say that my half-French father didn't trust the French was, in some ways, an understatement. Not only did he not trust their protestations, their written statements, or their solemn promises, he didn't trust their checks either.

He was once known to sell a clock business to a Frenchman. He insisted on payment in thousand-pound notes. He put them proudly on his desk, where they were inspected by the accountants. Even in those days thousand-pound notes were a curiosity.

He was telling the story of his sale of the clock business to me one day in the car.

"You know," he said, "they weren't annoyed when I said cash—they took it for granted. The French have quite a different view of business morality than we have."

At this moment we arrived at the pillared portico of his office.

"You can wait for me," he said, "I won't be long."

He mounted the shallow stairs, and through the glass doors, I could see him threading his way between the mirrored cabinets and the polished surfaces of the tables in the vestibule. It was a late November afternoon. The next second the light went on in his office. He took off his coat and hat, and sat down at his big desk. A man entered. Through the net curtains I could see my father and the man in discussion.

My father's hands were never still. With each sentence he made some gesture, either graceful or forcible, to emphasize or enforce the nub of his argument. Looking at him you would never for a moment have thought he was English.

History has a way of repeating itself. After the Second World War, my father took my mother on holiday to France, to Italy, and to Switzerland. He felt they needed a little relaxation after the rigors of the war.

But when my father arrived at Cannes, my mother took one look at the hotel and decided that she wasn't happy. My father took a look at my mother's face, and decided that if they stayed there he wouldn't be happy either. He gave the proprietor and everyone else he could find a piece of his mind. They transferred their cases and themselves to the Carlton. It seemed a pretty good hotel to them. After all, at their age, they argued, they were entitled to a few of life's little comforts. As my father repeated to me, "The best is always the cheapest in the end."

"Odd thing," said my mother on her return from this holiday, "in the train coming home, your father was talking French, as usual."

My mother did not disapprove of my father talking French when it was to buy things or order meals, but she was not so keen on his having chatty conversations with Frenchmen, because she did not speak French and felt out of it.

"This Frenchman," said my mother in a puzzled voice, "was *laughing!*"

I looked up.

"What was he laughing about?"

"I have no idea," said my mother. "In any case, your father isn't funny."

"Perhaps he is funny in French," I said.

My mother looked very dubious. Once you have a reputation in my family, it is impossible to lose it. As far as my mother was concerned, my father wasn't funny. And he was staying not funny—both in French and in English.

In the hall of our house hangs the sepia Madonna. The original was painted in 1899 by someone called Bouchereau. There is a touch of pre-Raphaelite about it. The Madonna has a chiseled profile offset by lilies. It doesn't look so bad in sepia.

My father bought it on my first visit to Brussels. The shop where we found it was in a steep little street which ran along beside Ste Gudule. The last time I went to Brussels, I saw that the trams which once rattled so frighteningly down the hill had gone. The street had gone, too. But I still have the sepia Madonna.

11 ✌ ✌ ✌

The Silver Mirror

I was the eldest in my family, and so, in the course of nature, I grew up first. This was a definite disadvantage. When I was already seventeen my next sister, Suzanne, was only twelve, my brother was nine, and Judith was four. We were all born in successive leap years. What that proves I have no idea, except that, as far as I was concerned, it was a definite handicap. I was the only young lady in a house of children. And I found myself the odd girl out.

My father, charmed and attracted as he was by children of all ages, was baffled by me. He couldn't understand why I wanted different things from my brother and sisters. They were perfectly happy playing around, getting dirty, tearing about in the fields with the dogs—why on earth did I want to go to dances or films in London? As we lived in the country, five miles from the station, it put him out.

My mother became my staunch ally. The great thing was not to let my father know I was going out—until I had already gone. It was then too late. They couldn't leave me at the station.

My mother could then plead the necessity of coming and fetching me.

Modern teen-agers think they have something to grumble about. I listen to their complaints about their parents with a smile. They simply don't know what they are talking about. My father was an Edwardian, and what was more, he was an Edwardian who was half French. If teen-agers want a worthy opponent, they should try taking that one on. That would be something to wipe the smiles right off their faces. That would really give them a complex, that would.

Modern parents are wrong, too. It is useless trying to be pally with one's children. There was no question of my father's chumming it up with me. The relationship was on a simple basis. He was right and I was wrong, and as long as I lived in his house, I was going to toe the line.

My idea was quite the opposite. I was quite determined to have my own way, and if I couldn't get it by fair means, then I would plot with my mother some more devious means of achieving the same result.

While I was still at school, this fundamental difference of approach between my father and myself was not apparent, but as soon as I left school it quickly became obvious.

As soon as that day arrived, my father decided that I better learn to do something. Once I had reached an age when I could earn some sort of a living, even if it was only enough to pay for my clothes, then I'd better get out and do it.

There was one thing about my father's attitude to women: he never treated them like fools. From an early age we always argued with him on a level. If we scored a good debating point against him, he would laugh delightedly. It gave him a kick to realize that he had sired a bunch who were worthy opponents.

However, my father's liberal attitude about women had its disadvantages. He wasn't going to have them hanging about the house waiting for Prince Charming to come along.

Earlier in my career he had wanted me to go to Oxford. But the idea of sticking out another two years of nuns first had horrified me, and I had gone to Brussels for a year instead. Once the idea of getting out and earning my living, or even some pin money, was mooted, I began to see that my decision had its disadvantages.

"All my friends from school are going to St. James' Secretarial College," I said hopefully. A little ladylike shorthand and typing was what I fancied.

He sent for the prospectus.

"If you think I'm going to pay a hundred guineas for you to learn shorthand and typing you have got another think coming," said my father.

My mother persuaded him to go and look at Queen's Secretarial College. We paid it a visit. We looked all round. My father seemed interested. He was even quite nice to the head woman. He looked with interest at the classrooms. He inquired into the curriculum. Everybody was happy and sociable. We reached the front door.

"How much did you say it was?" asked my father bluntly.

The head woman mentioned the price with a little cough which indicated that these were the kind of things which people did not usually take into account—the *atmosphere* was the main point. That, and the nice girls.

My father listened to the price with interest. He gave a snort.

"I think I'm in the wrong business," he said abruptly, and

we went out into the street. I was blushing with shame.

The upshot of all this was that I was sent to Pitman's where my mother and father had been before me, and my father bought me a small Austin Seven. My mother had maneuvered him into this position. The Austin cost a hundred pounds. I lost the refinement of Queen's, but I did get a car. And I got a certain amount of freedom. A limited amount of freedom. I could get about in the car, but unfortunately, my father had a much larger and faster car, and he, in turn, could get about after me. And he did.

On other occasions, as I nipped into the drive in my little blue car, I have seen him, clad in his dressing gown and slippers, opening the garage doors, full of the righteous rage of the outraged parent because it was half past ten, and I wasn't in.

Sometimes one almost got away with it. It was possible to turn off the car engine, and coast silently down the drive into the garage without disturbing him. But that wasn't the end. There were then other hazards. Canine hazards.

My mother was very fond of dogs. People were continually giving her dogs. The fact that we already had dogs did not seem to deter them. We had an Airedale called Bob and a mongrel called Bill; a London friend presented us with a Sealyham called John; we acquired a bobtailed sheepdog called Wilkie; and there was a charming red setter bitch called Lola. Individually, these dogs may have had charming natures; collectively, they made a formidable team.

In the village they were called the Massetts Pack. As soon as the gates were opened they streamed forth, inciting and exciting one another. Spreading terror and fury everywhere. The fact that no one knew us in the village, and that we weren't a family who were given to visiting vicars or villagers, made the dogs seem much worse, an unknown terror.

Most of the dogs didn't bite. But Bill the mongrel did. Like most of the underprivileged, he liked to get his own back. One day one of the villagers came to the front door. She came with a child. She came to complain. My father was sent for.

"Your dog bit my child," said the woman.

"When?" asked my father, looking grave and judicial.

"Yesterday."

"Where?"

"In the drive."

"I mean on the child," said my father testily.

The woman gave my father a look. If he didn't believe her, he'd asked for it. She took the child's knickers down and turned the child, bottom up, towards my father. There it was, a large round blue bite on the fair surface.

I must say my father looked a bit put out. It wasn't often he was disconcerted. He hastily pulled down the child's dress and gave the woman a clean pound note.

When I speak of canine hazards to the nocturnal breaking and entering of my father's house, I am not speaking lightly of chimeras, but of real-life dogs with long teeth, which they were prepared to use.

The dogs were locked up in the kitchen. Although this was the best way of getting into the house, it had all the disadvantages. It was very dark and overfull of dogs. You could poke your head round the door, and call softly in a coaxing voice, "Bob! Bill! Wilkie!" but the difficulty was that some of the dogs did not believe it was you. The mongrel, Bill, was not the kind of dog who was easily taken in. He would start to bark and then the whole pack would be at it. And before I knew where I was, there was my father, in his inevitable dressing gown, bellowing nearly as loudly as the dogs.

Even if you did manage to stop them barking, you ran the hazard of one of them taking a casual snack off your leg as you made off in the darkness.

A less noisy entrance to the house could be effected through the drawing-room windows. But it was more difficult. It needed a boy friend to lift you over the flower bed, and up to the latticed window. It was just too high to negotiate on one's own. Fortunately I was a slim little thing in those days, and boy friends were not reluctant to pop me through the drawing-room windows over the flowers. I tell you, the old song "Tiptoe Through the Tulips" had a real meaning for me when I was young.

Occasionally, some officious person, like Nanny, had decided to lock the inside of the drawing-room door. Then the fat was in the fire. I had to get out of the drawing-room window without the help of the loving arms of my current boy friend, and brave the snarling pack of dogs just the same.

When I did meet my father on my nocturnal prowlings, it was quite an encounter. He alternated between shouting and roaring, or being very quiet. Both angles terrified me. Between the roarings and the silences, and the barking of the dogs, he would threaten to take my car away.

Occasionally, I would ask boy friends down to lunch on Sunday, or they would come to dinner in the evening. He didn't seem to like the look of them. Generally, he tried to pretend they weren't there. I know that no one is quite good enough for one's daughter, but I don't think this was my

THE SILVER MIRROR

father's attitude. He just took one look at them and decided
they were fools, dolts, or mugwumps. Possibly some of them
were, but he didn't even give them a chance to speak in their
own defense. They were labeled as soon as they came in the
front door. Guilty until proved innocent. The French judicial
method.

My car was another source of fury to my father. When I was
eighteen there were no official driving tests and so I was taught
to drive at home. By my father. That was a mistake. He roared
at me so much that I used to let in the clutch with a jolt. The
little car would jump all over the road, like a frog, with my
father using frightful language, grabbing the wheel, and hanging on to the hand brake like mad. It was apparent that we
weren't getting on very fast. My mother took over. She taught
me to drive with patience, and soon I was bowling along the
road happily. Free to come and go at I pleased. I rather fancied
myself. I wore berets on the back of my head and thought I
looked like Greta Garbo. Snapshots prove that I didn't.

I bowled along the road, and sometimes I bowled off. The
lanes were narrow, the Austin Seven was very light, and a
sudden braking could send you into the ditch, and did.

My father was maddened by my driving. Every time I had
the most reasonable contretemps, like backing into a tree, or
knocking into the garage wall, a ban on driving would be
mentioned.

"She's a menace!" he would roar at my mother. "You didn't
know what you were doing when you taught her to drive!"

Basically he felt that if only he himself had taught me to
drive I would have managed better. He told my mother this.
She gave him one of her looks.

"If *you'd* taught her to drive she would have had a *nervous breakdown,*" said my mother.

Occasionally there were good reasons for my father's fury about my driving. Like the time I gently ran into a young man's car on Brighton Front, and made a large hole in the radiator of my car.

The young man was attractive. He couldn't understand why I was so worried. He towed me home. He had a large flashy car, and we made a sad procession as we wended our way all the fifteen miles from Brighton Front to the front door of the house.

My father was looking out of the window. The towrope had not escaped his eye.

We rang the bell. The young man came into the hall. He was easy, pleasant, debonair. There was not a cloud in *his* sky. My knees were knocking together.

"What has happened to my daughter's car?" said my father ominously.

"Nothing much," said the young man. "Radiator stove in. We'll soon fix that—my father owns a chain of garages. Rather fortunate, eh?"

My father's face told me he took the opposite point of view.

This shows there are more ways of meeting young men than being introduced to them at dances.

The car was repaired. I went out with the young man. But his conversation was limited. Mostly about cars. Cars had brought us together. The same subject parted us.

When I was twenty-one I got engaged. This suited my father much better. He liked my fiancé. He was the only young man he had ever deliberately asked down to the house, off his own bat. He was the kind of young man my father could talk to.

By this time we had moved nearer to the town. We were within walking distance of the bus route. I could nip home by the last train without further contretemps.

But even being engaged did not prove to be so easy after a while. There were dances in London. My father did not like my staying up in London for the night. He felt uneasy. It was not the kind of thing which happened in his day.

Then there were week-ends. We only had one car by this time. The Austin had worn out and had not been replaced. As an engaged couple, we had no money to buy a car because we were saving up to get married. So we were usually out in my father's car. Generally when he wanted it.

Or else we were too late back from the cinema. Fathers in my day had an uncanny instinct about what time the cinemas closed, and how long it took to drive back from Brighton. Explanations were regarded with the deepest suspicion.

I used to get into righteous rages.

My poor mama was subjected to rantings and ravings from both sides. I had quite a temper myself in those days. I used really to let my mother have it—about my father. My mother was much too tactful to tell him what I said about him behind his back. I was much too frightened of him to tell him the truth to his face. The political set-up was confused.

None of this affected my father.

The duty of children was to be happy in their homes. He knew where his own duty lay, and it was to protect the virtue of his daughter. He was, after all, the *père de famille*. If things were a little unpleasant temporarily, everything would settle down, once his eldest daughter learned to behave in what he considered to be a reasonable fashion. He knew what was best for her. Fathers always did.

The engaged couple had other views. Beneath the fair smiling surface of family relations, revolt smoldered. He wasn't going to get away with it. They would have something to say.

The cause of the outbreak came one Whitsun holiday. The idea was mooted that we should go to Brussels to see my sister, who was at school there. We thought it would be fun to go abroad together for ten days or so and see my old school. It would be gay being abroad, almost like a honeymoon. My father had already had just that same idea. He refused to let us go.

I was so angry when I heard his decision that I retired to my room and kicked the furniture. I also kicked my best hat. All around the room.

"If I wanted to be a slut," I said furiously to my mother, who was the amused witness of these histrionics, "I could just as easily be a slut in London! I don't have to go to Brussels to do it!"

She agreed that this was true. But my father didn't see it that way. I wasn't going to Brussels and that was that.

So we had a nice holiday in Cornwall, staying with my future parents-in-law. I have never forgotten that holiday. It was June. The arum lilies were high in the cottage gardens, and the cliffs were covered with sea thrift. Maybe Brussels wouldn't have been so nice. But we didn't see it that way. The revolt had not been quenched. It still rumbled on.

We were at the end of our tether. We would run away and get married quietly. We would take a furnished flat. We would live in digs. All these were fairly revolutionary ideas in my young days. A young man was expected to provide a home (with furniture) before he married. Yes, we were desperate, we decided. We were going to elope. Naturally all this, interspersed with sentimental, consoling interludes, took some time to discuss, and it was four o'clock in the morning before we went up the stairs to bed. At least I nipped up quietly. My fiancé was a few minutes after me. Being of a romantic nature, he had been out in the garden smelling the summer scent of jasmine which grew on the wall of the house.

When he finally went up to bed, he heard a soft step on the stairs. His girl. He would surprise her. He had his cigarette lighter in his hand. He flicked it on in the darkness. A large angry face appeared in the flicking light of the flame—my father's.

Neither of them said anything. They couldn't think of anything to say.

Wedding pictures prove that we didn't elope. We got married in church. I was given away by my father, in white satin, carrying lilies. We had a large wedding, and our first holiday abroad together was our honeymoon.

But it's odd to think that if it hadn't been for my father I should never have met my future husband. He was learning to type at Pitman's. Just like me. He lent me an eraser. His father was economizing, too. Just as well, really, that I didn't learn to type with all those refined friends of mine.

The silver mirror is a relic of my engagement. It was the first thing we ever bought for our future home. We bought it in the Lanes at Brighton for twelve and sixpence, one day when we had pinched my father's car.

When I showed it to my father, he didn't like the look of it.

CHEAPEST IN THE END

"Just an Edwardian survival," he said.

At the time I thought that applied to him, and I was a little narked. I still think it's rather a pretty mirror.

The valuer says it's worth twelve pounds ten.

12 ✄✄✄

Whittaker's Almanac

To those people who take money seriously, money is a very serious subject. Banks, insurance companies, all the places where money in the abstract is taken seriously, are like temples built to the worship of money. Walled and floored in marble, tricked out with mahogany and plate glass, their *décor* proclaims the high seriousness of money.

Sometimes one wonders why there is not a little temple set up to the worship of money at the entrance to these palaces of its cult. In an alcove would be set a bar of gold, and before it would burn a perpetual flame, and as the worshippers entered the temple they would bow low, and sprinkle a few grains of incense on the flames. The perfume of the incense would rise up like the perfume of money itself.

My father didn't take money seriously. There was only one thing he liked to do about money, and that was to spend it.

It was an attitude which was not shared by most of his co-directors on the board. They had ideas which coincided with orthodox banking practice and sound finance. In their view, every day was a rainy day and had to be prepared for.

As a result of this clash of views, board meetings were not the happiest days in the yearly calendar for my father. Although he was managing director, he was not chairman and he hadn't control of the company, so he was forced into conflict with people who had different views about the value of money. They liked it as an abstract subject. Money was a fine thing in itself, and the beauty of a balance sheet, or the turn of a phrase on an agenda, really meant a great deal to them. They took money as perhaps it should be taken, as a very serious subject.

"Mugwumps," said my father. "Mugwumps, the lot of them! About as much brains as my backside."

He was inclined to be forthright in a Gallic way when roused.

"Bloody clerks," he would add, just in case we had missed the point.

His idea was that the business was important. Balance sheets were all very well in their way, and a good credit balance was a nice shot in the arm for any business. But what he liked to feel was that the thing was surging forward. He liked getting large orders, and he liked seeing schemes being put in hand.

When it came to questions about money, he became very angry. Basically he felt that people—and this included his board—ought to be satisfied to see the business spinning round. He couldn't be bothered with all the details about whether it was making a profit or not.

Imagination, drive, vision, these were the things which governed him. Not balance sheets. Balance sheets were for clerks. He had no time for clerks. And no time for balance sheets either. They bored him. He found it difficult to concentrate on the report and accounts.

It all looked a bit dry to him.

Accounts had never been his strong point, not even at the very beginning of his career. He had been sacked from his first job as a clerk, for adding up wrong and making a hole in the ledger. Ironically, the firm which sacked him was the very firm where later he became managing director.

Basically he had not changed. He was still making holes in the ledger.

"Why am I always plagued with fools?" my father would mutter darkly, coming home from some board meeting which hadn't gone too well.

It wasn't that he wanted to make a loss, or that he didn't like doing well; he did. It was just that he could not understand the attitude of the other people on the board. The kind of gentlemen who bustle in and out of the temples built to the worship of money, taking it seriously, removing their bowler hats when they speak of it. Money was not a serious subject with my father, except when his bank statement came in. Then his cries of rage filled the house. My mother usually liked to keep out of his way when the first of the month came round.

None of his codirectors had the faintest idea about business, according to him. They were always counting the cost. That wasn't the way to get on.

His idea was to think up some imaginative new scheme of expansion.

"That would mean a bank loan," the directors would say nervously.

"Why not?" asked my father.

Give him a loan to raise from a bank, and he was in his element. While the devotees of sound finance regarded banks with the awe which they liked to exact, my father felt they were there to help him. His attitude towards a bank was friendly, but far from reverent. He felt that, in general, banks were instituted to lend money, and that there was no reason why they shouldn't lend it to him. He usually justified their confidence in him, for he was a dead honest man, and they knew it. So there was absolutely no reason why they shouldn't lend him money.

So they did.

This result sometimes confounded his codirectors. They felt there was some flaw in their thinking, if a man with no money sense could get money for projects out of banks so easily. It did not seem to be quite fair.

When we were first married, and my husband was a reporter in Fleet Street, we were extremely hard up. The bank was getting sticky.

"Quite simple," said my father. "The manager is clearly a mugwump. Take your overdraft elsewhere."

So we did. The bank manager was quite upset. It had never occurred to him that we might walk out.

My father's life in business was not peaceful. Nothing seemed to be simple for him. Nothing seemed to run smoothly. There were constant squalls. He always seemed to be surrounded by difficulties, by the dust of disputes, and by the shrill clash of argument.

Board meetings were conducted in an atmosphere of high debate. His quick, thumbnail sketches of his directors gave us a gallery of portraits which would not have disgraced Hogarth. Thin-faced, narrow-minded, evil-hearted men, with nothing to recommend them, seemed to abound.

One got the impression of a polished table surrounded by a

sea of pinched disapproving faces, the kind of set-up which would not have disgraced the Inquisition, or the agents of Cecil under the Catholic Persecution.

And there, confronting his torturers, was my father. The noble pure-hearted knight. Someone who only wanted to do the best for the business, and was prevented by his diabolical cabal. My father would come back from his encounters with his board seething with rage, red-faced, angry, and frustrated.

There was only one flaw in the touching picture which he drew of his persecution. The things he admitted to having said. They were not the kind of things which most people like to hear.

The board which confronted my father have long since retired, or died. Whether they had indeed any of the characteristics of perfidy and chicanery which my father was wont to indicate, I must doubt. But it seemed that their qualities of underhand dealing, of ganging up against him, or combining with shareholders to thwart his simplest wishes, would not have disgraced Stalin's henchmen.

Once, and once only, his deepest suspicions were justified. They tried to get rid of him.

One man in particular, now dead, decided that he would have a freer hand without my father, and so a real cabal was started to push my father out. In the end, it was a question of my father resigning—or one man. One or the other.

My father was then in his late fifties. It was not possible for him to start in a new business. And his optimistic nature had not indicated to him any necessity of saving. His position was not only his livelihood, it was his life. It was his background, it was the support of his family.

He was a fighter and he decided to fight. His back was really against the wall.

Being a man of absolute integrity, my father had no use for the byways of business. The bribe, the half-truth, the concealed loss, were things which he despised. That others were not so scrupulous never occurred to him, and if they wanted bribes for services rendered, then so much the worse for them. He wasn't prepared to copy them.

I don't know much about the formation of companies, but I do know that sometimes free shares are dished out at the time of their formation, or re-formation, shares which afterwards may become worth good money. This is part of what is known as "getting in on the ground floor."

At the time of the rearrangement of my father's company money, or shares, or both, had been demanded for services rendered. My father had agreed. He would not have taken money himself, but if money was what people wanted, then they must have it, if saving the business was the objective. In the thirties, many people's jobs depended on a project like that.

For some reason, which I now forget, this particular changing of money or shares was illegal. It was some technicality to do with the fact that directors could not take payment for doing something from which they would afterwards benefit. The legal angles of the thing are now lost in the mists of distance. When it comes to pure legalities, honesty and dishonesty are separated by a hair's breadth.

The final encounter between my father and the enemy took place at the Dorchester. The enemy had set the venue. As my father walked through the doors into the vestibule, he realized that everything depended on this final throw. Tomorrow he could be a pauper without a job.

He walked up to the settee under the soft lighting where the man sat. He looked at him. They greeted one another. Anyone looking at them ordering their whiskies would have thought they were two business acquaintances meeting in order to discuss things to their mutual profit.

After a preliminary exchange of news about the health of their families, their children, the man spoke, and with his first words made the gross tactical error which caused his downfall.

He offered to give my father back the bribe.

"I shall have to speak to my lawyer," said my father instantly.

He walked around the corner. He went into one of the phone booths. But he didn't ring anyone up. He stayed there for a couple of minutes and then he went back with a ponderous expression on his face.

"What did he say?" demanded the man.

Like those clouds in bad religious paintings which contain a good carload of saints, the bribe seemed to hang palpably above their heads, like some living thing.

My father looked dubious.

"Nothing much we can do," he said.

He made no mention of prosecutions, or legal processes; he said nothing more. He left all to the dramatic implications of the moment, and the overhanging cloud of bribery.

"He feels I should resign?" queried the man.

My father gave a Gallic *moue*. An expression of the mouth which indicated that he would not have suggested it himself, but if the fellow felt that resigning would save his face, then, reluctantly, my father would agree to his resigning. They looked at one another.

"I'll send in my letter in the morning," said the enemy.

"Very well," said my father.

He got up, bowed, and then turning round, made the only little remark of revenge which he allowed himself.

"The board will miss you," he said.

In spite of modern ideas to the contrary, honesty does, sometimes, pay off.

"From the first moment to the last I never had the slightest doubt about winning," said my father later.

He never had any doubts about winning the First World War, either.

Apart from the dolts, fools, and crooks which he allegedly encountered while carrying out his business, my father also had another load of dolts, fools, and crooks to deal with. These were his clients.

In addition to being sorely tried by his board, my father was also sorely tried by his customers.

Unfortunately for my father, the antique and decorating business is mostly concerned with people who already have money. And people who have money like everyone to take them seriously. Tribute must be paid to their moneyed state. Their slightest wish must be gravely considered. The fact that they have money to waste on the trimmings of life gives them a good deal of scope. At the drop of a check book, armies of subservient designers, decorators, and seekers for exquisite this-and-that's can be summoned. And oppressed at will.

I don't know how it is now, but way back in the thirties people who spent money on furnishing and decorating spent a very great deal of money indeed. They ordered entire houses to be done up regardless of cost. They had the money, and my father's designers had the taste.

In the studio, exquisite water-color drawings would be made, depicting rooms which could be created at the wave of the two words, "go ahead." And from the drawing boards arose paneled libraries, padded-silk bedrooms with gilded French furniture, or exquisite drawing rooms in the Spanish style. It was as simple as that.

But, like my father when his bank statement came in, his rich customers did not like the look of the accounts when they were rendered. Following on the heels of the creation of these splendid rooms came the complaints. And when really rich people complain, they complain very loudly. Especially the women.

Rich women don't mind how much they complain. They have plenty of leisure, and complaining fills some of their free time. It also gives them something to bore their friends with at dinner parties, making a nice change from diets and divorces. Rich women are also not too particular about what little rearrangements of the truth they may employ, when they do complain.

My father's clients sometimes had the crooked capacity which he encountered in various other phases of his business career. They borrowed antique furniture and smashed it, subsequently declaring that it had been delivered broken, in this way neatly throwing the blame on the porters, who could not hit back.

They ordered needlework chairs and returned them later, complaining that the colors did not suit their rooms. They omitted to mention the wine stains which had ruined the needlework.

Those who think of the antique and decorating business as a nice gentlemanly profession probably forget that, when decorating rooms, the clients are usually not gentlemen, either in the sexual or social sense of the word.

My father had no great use for the really rich, especially not for his rich women clients. Like his board of directors, they took money seriously.

"It's impossible to be really rich and remain sane," my father would declare after some foray into the jungle of his clientele. "The only way to be rich is to do things for other people. Most don't."

The only very rich women my father had any use for were Annie, Lady Cowdray, and Lady Louis Mountbatten.

The rest of them just represented to him a series of complaints. Complaints about the colors of paints, complaints about the shade of silks specially woven in France, complaints about murals specially commissioned from artists. Complaints, in fact, about everything from the placing of a wall light to the knocking in of a single nail.

Complaints were countered in depth, first the foreman, then the man in charge of the designing of the whole scheme, then, after flank skirmishes with artists, painters, soft-furnishing men, the final arbiter, my father. The complaint would arrive on his desk.

If the complaint seemed justified, the fat was in the fire. My father was not content with superficial explanations of what had gone wrong. He would send for everybody, from the exquisite young gentleman who had talked the client into having bottle-green walls, down to the man who had actually had the temerity to mix and apply the paint.

A specially serious complaint about dilatory workmen reached my father one day. He sent for the foreman on the job. He always had very charming foremen, and they had pleasant old-fashioned manners which went with the legend on the portico outside which said, "Established in 1770."

"I have a complaint from Lady X about slow progress," said my father. He raised his eyes solemnly from his paper. Behind his large eighteenth-century desk, looking over his glasses, his gray hair offset by the Adam-green background of the room, my father was quite a formidable sight. He could have been the squire in his library.

He looked sternly at the foreman. The reputation of the firm was at stake. Service was the one thing, above all, which they prided themselves on.

It was a solemn moment.

"Well, sir—" began the foreman.

"I don't want any excuses," said my father. "I want to know exactly *why* they are complaining."

"Well, sir," the foreman repeated, "by the time Lady X has taken the pony and trap through the dining room, it's a bit difficult for the men to get going again."

The foreman was looking respectful, but not unaware of the farcical nature of his explanation.

"Horse and trap?"

"Yes, sir," said the foreman. "You see, it's a mews house, and they are still using part of it for its original purpose."

My father said no more.

Taking it all in all, my father had a very stormy business life. He had a positive genius for unearthing new seams of mugwumps, fools, dolts, and crooks. They were on his board, they constituted most of his clients, they were also in the National Liberal Club, and they were even in the hierarchy of the Church itself. He was a miner of real genius when it came to unearthing fools and crooks.

It has since, of course, occurred to everyone that my father was inclined to be quarrelsome.

The only thing I have which came from my father's office in those far-off stormy days is *Whittaker's Almanac*.

This has a heavy section devoted to the peerage, baronetage, and knightage, together with the modes of addressing them. It was for the use of my father's secretary when writing letters of apology to clients. I don't suppose that it is much needed now, when the richest clients usually only need a "dear sir or madam."

The emphasis has shifted.

13 ✌✌✌

The Steel Claw

In every house there is a cupboard which seems to attract a series of tools, pots of paints, and tins of screws and nails. In our cupboard there is a steel claw. This is a weapon used by porters for opening packing cases. It is a relic of one of the numerous moves undertaken by my family in the thirties.

I can remember my father using it.

He was proud of his hands and used them delicately. But not even his family, who admired him, could say that he was really handy with tools. He was a man who was greatly thwarted by inanimate objects.

Inanimate objects ganged up to annoy my father. Garage doors stuck, car tires deliberately developed punctures, bathroom cupboards fell off walls. There was something spiteful about the behavior of inanimate objects where my father was concerned.

It was not that he was not good with his hands. He could be if he put his mind to it, but he did not intend to, because the conspiracy of the inanimate objects which surrounded him

133

absolutely maddened him. They did it on purpose. He regarded them with an eye which did not wish them well.

He did not suffer this usurped rule of inanimate objects gladly. His cries of baffled rage and fury against them filled the house like some scene out of an old-time melodrama. Henry Irving in "'The Bells" could not have done better than my father, with evil glances, agonized expressions, and looks of scorn, when confronted with some nail which had had the temerity to fall off the wall.

He was not the kind of man who likes to be handy about the house, who keeps oiled tools in rows and knows where everything is. When asked to do something by my mother, he parried the suggestion, but if finally forced into a corner and asked point-blank to "do it today," his reply was to appear with a disgruntled expression and a hammer.

A hammer was the weapon which, my father felt, was suited to most jobs in the house. A good sound blow with the hammer was the answer to any problem. The delinquent object either went back into place, or broke. Either way, it was a solution. He had the same attitude to business problems. A good sound hammer blow would solve them either way.

My mother was not deterred by my father's lack of love for jobs about the house. She was an optimist. Some day, she felt, Clemmy would be one of those men who were always running up little shelves, or painting the larder. She never learned. Basically, my father, with his artistic streak, was very bad material for this role. His idea about household jobs was to get someone else to do them.

When he did them himself, the mess was indescribable. He would never clear anything up. His activities did not need a

Sherlock Homes to piece them together. Hammers, nails, rawl-plugs—everything he had used on a job remained where he had thrown them. If my mother protested, his reply was succinct.

"If you wanted a bloody lackey, you should have married one."

My mother's mouth would take on a prim governessy expression. This expression had a certain awful significance of its own. Like the look on the face of an Egyptian cat, it denoted that her dignity was sinister but sacred.

My father usually tried to ignore this expression. If he was angry enough, he would throw his hammer down and walk off. If she was even more angry, she would turn on her heel, wrapped in an icy silence, and make a *grande dame* exit. My mother is small, but her icy silences are the iciest I know. On occasions they have been known to intimidate my father. And he was not a man who was easy to intimidate.

Another thing my father was plagued by was an unknown character called "some damn fool." "Some damn fool" left garage doors open, "some damn fool" laid bicycles deliberately in the drive so that when he swept in with a flourish he ran over them. I can see him now picking the bones of my brother's bicycle out of his Buick's wheels.

"What damn fool left this bicycle here?" he roared. The particular damn fool needed was not at hand. Mark was out sailing.

"Some damn fool" was a well-known and actually well-liked character in our family. Often by a judicious silence, "some damn fool" could take the blame for garden taps left running, tennis nets which had been left out in the rain, cars which had been left in gear, and dogs which had been let out.

Sunday was a good day for finding damn fools. With every-one at home there was no limit to the damage they could do. There was the Sunday morning when my father was sitting in his elegant drawing room, surrounded by bowls of sweet peas and at peace with the world. "Some damn fool" could and did easily interrupt this idyllic picture.

He looked up, and out into the garden.

A strange sight met his eye. There on the lawn, capering between the clipped yew hedges, what did he see? Nothing less than Bob, the Airedale, sporting in the sun, with a leg of mutton in his happy jaws.

"What damn fool let that dog get the joint?"

The combination of his Sunday lunch being ruined, and the activities of the damn fool who had let the dog make off with it, provoked my father to a Jovelike rage. He flung open the French windows, and set off in hot pursuit of the dog. Bob, a cheerful, friendly creature, liked nothing better than a good game. He pranced round the lawn, ready for fun. It was not until the dog made off towards the orchard that my father cornered him near the potting shed. He returned in grim silence with the leg of lamb, bearing it with heavy tread to-wards the kitchen.

Someone was going to get into trouble. I ran upstairs. I was not anxious to be embroiled. My father's disputes had a way of involving anybody who was in sight or earshot. Like a huge stone hurled into a pool, the eddies might easily catch up with the paddlers on the fringe.

Among the inanimate objects which plagued my father were cars. He had very little patience with them. If they went wrong, he had absolutely no use for them. He liked cars to be large, fast, *and* going. There was no question of them breaking down, as far as my father was concerned. If they did, he got rid of them.

There was a time when my mother talked him into having a smaller car, on the grounds of economy. The garage man was soothing about the car. My father was not at all sure about it. He was a large man, and it did not suit his dignity to have to fold himself into a small car. What he liked was a large, fast Buick. However, he had not had a very good year and so my mother was on a good wicket. He bought the small car.

Some designer had had a brain wave about that car. The brain wave was an automatic self-starter. The only trouble was that the starter would take it into its head to start when the engine was already running. We were driving into Brighton to the theater one evening, when suddenly, near the Palace Pier, where the traffic swirled round, the self-starter decided to show its paces. With regular monotony it started to self-start above the noise of the engine.

With a grim look on his face, my father got out of the car. His expression was set. In his hand was the usual hammer. He pulled up the bonnet of the car, and gave the offending part a ferocious blow with the hammer. The self-starter stopped self-starting. It knew its place.

My father gave a snort of satisfaction, and folded himself back into the car.

"That settles it," he said. "The damned thing goes tomorrow." He had won the battle of the small car versus the large one.

The reason my father liked fast cars was quite simply that he liked driving fast. Also he was not keen to see anyone in front of him on the road.

He was fond of pointing out that he had been driving for thirty, or was it forty, years, and had never had an accident. I never quite decided whether this was due to his quick wits, or to the evasion tactics taken by others.

A drive with my father was not devoid of incident. On the roads damn fools abounded. They bred like rabbits. They were round every corner. They lurked at every crossroads. And between encounters with damn fools, one had periods of sheer fright at the simple speed of the car. Bounding at eighty-five across Walton Heath, or doing eighty on the Birdham straight, one arrived white and shaking. Protests from passengers were not to be considered. He knew what he was doing, he said.

Apart from encounters with damn fools, there were also the natural hazards of the road, such as corners, narrow hump-backed bridges, and sharp dips in the road, which were clearly the fault of uninspired Council planning. They were deliberately put in my father's way to reduce his speed. But they were not going to succeed. My father ignored them.

When not frightening his passengers to death, my father liked to do people good turns. He had a kind heart and liked to give pleasure. Near us in the country lived old Lady Jane. She was the daughter of some Irish earl and her properties had been burned in the Troubles. She was an elegant old lady, and a great friend of the family. My father offered to take her for a drive. She had not a car of her own and a little expedition would amuse her, my father pointed out.

A drive down to West Sussex was decided on. Perhaps we might get as far as Petworth for tea. We set off at a fine spanking pace. It was a bright sunny day, the roads were clear. We were not in a hurry. But my father was.

Lady Jane was dressed for motoring; round her neck were swathed a few layers of mauve and gray veiling. On her head was a violet-filled toque. Underneath the toque peered a pair of frightened old eyes. They were eyes which could not concentrate on the flying landscape. They were fixed on the road ahead. The road which seemed to beckon and incite my father to further bursts of speed.

Just beyond Horsham, at an even speed of fifty, my father sped happily over a humpbacked bridge. Old Lady Jane bounced smartly off the back seat, hitting her head on the roof of the car. She was a little quiet for the rest of the journey, and refused food when we stopped for tea.

When we arrived back safely at Lady Jane's cottage, she got out of the car and thanked my father in her old-fashioned, over-formal way. Then she walked down the garden path with her daughter. She was leaning heavily on her daughter's arm.

My father looked after her.

"Old Lady Jane seems to look much older these days," he said sympathetically.

I was not perhaps as concerned as I might have been about the buoyant elastic qualities of poor Lady Jane. But life has a way of catching up with you. I hit the roof of a Buick, a much later model, in exactly the same way on the same humpbacked bridge, some ten years later. I happened to be pregnant at the time with my first child.

In response to the pleas of my mother, my father did slow down then. However, it was his private opinion that pregnancy had made me a little hysterical. One had to make allowances for hysterical women.

The humpbacked bridge is still there. I can only hope that there are no modern motorists like my father.

It was not only on the roads that my father found damn fools. In his life there was infinite scope for the proliferation of damn fools. One was my grandfather, known as the "old boy."

The "old boy" was always doing mad, demented things, according to my father. My grandfather was very old; in the thirties he was already approaching ninety. When one looks back, he was a phenomenon. He was bright, agile, and on the beam. But he was no phenomenon to my father.

The old boy would break up my father's cigarettes to smoke in his pipe. The old boy would upset the servants by being too sympathetic. Now I think back on it, my grandfather lived a life in himself. He usually sat upstairs with Nanny, and I suppose he liked a good chat. But the old boy's little chats maddened my father. The old boy wasted the time of everyone in the house, according to my father, from the maid in the kitchen to the gardener who was supposed to be cutting the lawn.

If my grandfather was no phenomenon to my father, my father was certainly no phenomenon to my grandfather. The trouble was that they were both equally strong characters, and not much quarter was given. After an argument my grandfather would stalk out, usually hitting his head on something. Although my grandfather was a short man, it was astonishing how often he hit his head on things. His head seemed to be the most ubiquitous head in the business.

Another thing which annoyed my father was my grandfather's feet. They always seemed to be in the wrong place. He would descry my grandfather's footprints in such places as newly planted rosebeds, or on newly polished floors. Man Friday had nothing on my grandfather.

My grandfather had no way with inanimate objects either. If my father was plagued by them, they baffled my grandfather completely. His musician's hands, knotted with rheumatism, found it impossible to shut doors properly, or even to put a glass back in a cupboard without breaking it. This was not because he was old, but merely that he could not do anything practical. The trail of damage left by my grandfather added to the plague of inanimate objects with which my father was constantly pestered.

Another object which was a constant source of anger to my father was his carving knife. He had a bit of a thing about carving knives, and was constantly buying new ones.

Sunday, and Sunday lunch, was a day of great ceremony. The French habit of the entire family gathering after Mass for a large and copious meal was strong in my father. In our case, of course, it was the usual Sunday joint.

It would be brought in by the maid. My mother always had maids from a convent orphanage. They were bright-faced girls, but when the joint was overdone or underdone, then they looked far from bright. Even a look at the outside of a joint would tell my father whether some maniac had ruined it.

Having examined the joint with an expert's eye, he would then pick up his knife. He would hold the blade up to the light. He wasn't sure about the joint but he would start to carve. No sooner had the blade been applied than he was aware that one at least of his fears had been confirmed.

"What damn fool has been using my carver?" he would roar.

Dead silence would ensue. Frightened faces would remain quite still.

"No one has been using your carver," my mother would say in her tiniest voice.

"Look at it!" my father would hold it out angrily. "Look at the blade! It looks more like a saw. Some bloody fool has been chopping mint with it!"

My mother never deigned to reply. The maid disappeared tactfully into the pantry. Although hungry, she thought it more judicious to wait until her lunch had been put through the hatch. There was no sense in staying in the bull ring when the picadors had been at work.

The silence in the dining room was then punctuated by regular strokes of the knife on the steel. When my father was satisfied with the sharpness of his knife he started to carve in earnest. Fortunately the joint was usually just right. Plates were filled and voices were raised.

Once his own plate was filled, and he had seen that everything was to his liking, my father relaxed. The moment of danger had passed. He would look round the table.

He was proud of his children. We were a good-looking lot in those days. I can say this because, being middle-aged, I know that it is all in the past. We were all dark, all lively, and all prepared to give battle to my father. On rare occasions this aspect of our characters did not so much appeal to him.

Occasionally some chance remark would annoy him. Although he had an appreciation of certain jokes, others would pass him by completely. Often the whole table, including my mother, would be laughing uproariously while he remained absolutely calm. Outside the joke. This did not worry him. It was obvious to him that his family had a very childish, and sometimes misplaced, sense of humor.

Occasionally the butt of the joke was himself. Apart from the inanimate objects in the house and garden which conspired to anger him, there were alien objects like misplaced pavements on which he could stub his foot.

When my mother laughed at him hopping round holding his foot, he would shout angrily, "I suppose you think people hurting themselves is a joke? I suppose it would have been even funnier if I had broken my damned ankle?"

The sight of a dignified, well-dressed man hopping round on one foot as if he had been stung by bees held no tragic overtones for us. My father limped on.

When I was young I often wanted to live in one of those families where everyone is demonstrably loving, where life has a wonderful timeless quality and goes rolling on in an orderly way. I saw myself as Miss Madeleine of the Manor.

In the ideal home of my imaginings kind old butlers and nurses abounded, and everyone was very calm, polite, and old-world. My father never fitted into this picture. In the Manor of my imaginings no one ever went near the kitchen. It was beneath them. It wasn't beneath my father.

"What is that bloody girl doing?" he roared one day. "Where are the damned boiled potatoes?"

No reply came from the kitchen. No reply came from the dining room either. He left the room and flung open the kitchen door.

One of his axioms was that if you wanted anything done, you had to bloody well do it yourself. He was doing just that.

"The hotplate won't heat," said the frightened girl who cowered beside the stove.

"What do you mean?" said my father.

He clapped his hand on to the hotplate. It lived up to its name. It was hot. He howled with pain.

Presently a procession appeared in the doorway. First came the maid bearing a dish of steaming boiled potatoes, and behind, like a priest carrying some sacred object, walked my father, with his injured hand in a jug of water. My sister and I burst into muffled giggles.

"You had better go out!" said my mother. She was not looking for trouble.

We left the table, we walked down the garden path and out into the lane. We were still laughing as a stentorian voice floated out across the hedges on the summer air.

"Everyone takes me for a bloody fool!" it roared. "I may be a fool, but I'm not a bloody fool!"

Everyone cherishes his little illusions.

14 ✦✦✦

Jane's Fighting Ships

THE letter lay on the hall table all the long winter afternoon. It was an official letter. It could have been income tax—the kind of letter one opens last. No one was to know that it announced the death of an only son. It announced the death of my brother.

He was twenty-two. Tall, extremely handsome, gay and clever, he had been given by his father all the worldly chances which he himself had missed. The letter ended all that. "H.M. Submarine Vandal has failed to return to base . . . their Lordships regretted . . ."

Their Lordships regretted that he was the only son of his mother, their Lordships regretted that he was the only brother of his sisters. Their Lordships regretted that his destruction was possible.

Their Lordships stated that his father should regard him as missing.

Films have commercialized emotions about the war. They have reduced to a cliché the destruction of youth. They have made heroism into a joke. They have translated deep, terrible experiences into a box-office success. The mechanical gabble cackles on, the spirit is dead—like my brother.

Mark was a materialist who died for an ideal he never expressed, a cynic who followed his religion faithfully, a vulgar young man who was pure.

Purity, ideals, faith—they look worn, greasy cards when you put them on the table with the bright new pack.

Tragedy, when it strikes a family, strikes it in depth. Each one suffers for himself, and he suffers for the others. It is a wound like a fishhook stuck in the flesh, tearing many different ways.

"Missing," said my father. "They wouldn't have said missing if they had no hope, would they?"

"Of course they wouldn't."

The echoes of my brother's voice came back to me—"I don't want to see 'after the war.' I don't think it is the sort of world I would like."

"Naturally," my father went on in a purposefully businesslike voice, "it all depends whether they were bombed, or mined, or whether there were any survivors."

It tore at the heart to hear him discussing the possibilities of his son's destruction as if it were a board meeting.

My mother did not weep. She did not cry out. She rocked herself about as if in terrible pain, as if the center of her guts had been mortally wounded. To see such a controlled woman so primitively stricken and to know of no drug or word that could relieve the pain was a grief beyond pain itself.

Judith lay in a darkened room when the news came. When the violent pains of the migraine had left her, she came down to the drawing room to find me sitting quietly weeping by the fire.

"For Christ's sake, stop sniveling," she said.

Other people's emotions are upsetting. I dried my eyes.

"He knew he wasn't going to come back," she said. "He told me so. It was only a question of how and when."

Her face had that strained look of acceptance which the young cultivated in those far-off days twenty years ago. It was a look compounded of the knowledge that death and mutilation might come, but that when it did one must not cry out or complain. One must accept that life was full of death.

A death in the family has two effects. To some it is like a leper's bell—it warns people to keep away. They like to leave you isolated in grief. Is there tragedy and destruction about? They don't want to hear about it. Is all flesh mortal? They don't want to be reminded of it. They give themselves the facile comfort that it would be much too upsetting for the family to see anyone so soon after the tragedy. They nod, they smile, they wave from a distance, but they don't ask you for drinks until it looks as if the first shock has passed, and there is no longer any chance of their being upset by secondhand grief. One has to be careful of one's feelings. There is no point in spreading the load.

The other way is to indulge in long condolence letters. To remind his family of the young man's past gallantries and medals, how he enjoyed sailing before the war, and now had gone out to sea never to come back, seems a useful occupation for pent-up feelings.

Useless to put "no letters please" in the paper. No one thinks it applies to them. So each letter is like a stabbing recollection of the past that will never come back.

A brief life is like a perfume from the past. A breath of happier, more hopeful time, when people knew that life was precious and death was possible.

To take out a packet of old letters, marked with the stamp "From H.M. Ship, Passed by Censor," is to step back into a time when the streets were full of destruction and hearts were full of resolution. It is like a "dissolve" in a film, and you are back in 1943, back with the old pain, and with the old hopes.

You listen again to your father's voice guessing the possibilities about the continuance of hope. And while he talks you can see Mark as a grinning boy at prep school with a handful of cups for running and winning the egg-and-spoon races. Cups presented by parents who liked to hear their names read out in grateful thanks.

You see your mother's sad, rigid face, and again, like a double exposure, you watch the young man setting the sails of his Sharpie in Itchenor harbor. Again you sit in the bows of the boat and you hear his voice: "I like to hear the lapping sound of the water." You both listen. An intense peace wells up in your heart. A peace blended from the blue of the day, the sound of the water, the friendliness of being together. A great gulp of happiness comes back across the years, distillation of a today which was happy. A today when tomorrow stretched limitlessly into a blue sky. A today when no one was dead, or disillusioned, and life had a great simplicity of purpose.

A today of pre-war. A time currently funny and to be mocked at. The French-window era, when neat maids brought banana sandwiches out onto lawns for tennis teas, when drawing rooms were full of prize sweet peas in glass bowls, and voices came clearly across the lawn, full of hope.

You open a drawer, and there, in the bottom of a box, lies a packet of large black hooks and eyes. Hooks and eyes which have proved to be more enduring than the young man who bought them in Gibralter in 1942.

A voice cried "Rabbits," and from a canvas bag poured a load of treasures, dress materials, cigarettes, sherry in gin bottles, silk stockings, and "Amour, Amour."

So many things had a great value and simplicity back in 1942. And the young man with the canvas bag chose his presents with care, bringing the things he knew were in short supply, to use the current phrase of 1942. It is hard to imagine a situation where a packet of bobby pins, or a card of hooks and eyes could be regarded as luxuries brought back from over a sea full of death. Yet there they are in the bottom of the drawer. Newey's Finest Hard Steel Wire All British Hooks and Eyes with the Extra Japanned Finish, as brightly japanned as ever. But he brought so many that they have never quite been used up. They have outlasted three work-baskets. Hard to remember a time when it was a sweet thought to be given a packet of hooks and eyes.

Hard to remember a time when you walked down Piccadilly with a tall naval officer, and his solitary ribbon, the George Medal, attracted as much attention from the girls as his tanned, handsome face and his bright gray eyes. Hard to remember groping your way round a dead, dark city with him, trying to find a restaurant which was only indicated by a tiny red illuminated sign which said "Open."

"Like a brothel," said Mark.

Hard to remember falling into the dustbins at Dolphin

Square because we had forgotten our torches.

Hard to remember the tarts in Jermyn Street drawing attention to themselves by using theirs.

Hard to remember the old jokes—his jokes. "Do you know the definition of utility knickers?" You shake your head. "One Yank and they're off."

Just very hard to remember the perfume of the past. Yet a sad, fat Negro pianist can bring it back. Fats playing "Honeysuckle Rose" can bring them back, those summers of long ago, can bring back the gay young man lying full length on the settee with the summer sounds of voices concerned with masts and sails, with spinnakers and the dangers of crossing the sand bar at low tide. Voices which found greater dangers than these before their echoes were stilled.

You walk down the village street at Itchenor today. It is full of Jaguars. The Sailing Club is smart. You can be photographed chatting on the Sailing Club lawn and appear in the *Tatler*. Everyone looks very correct. Very Lily-white.

But look up in the Club Bar and you don't see any little roll of honor of the young men who sailed there when it was not rated *Tatler* material. You don't see a roll call of the young man who went down as a rating in the *Hood,* or the other one who was sunk in an icy sea taking supplies to Murmansk. You don't like to be reminded that you might not be there drinking Plymouth, pink, if it had not been for the young men who sailed at the Club when it was not good *Tatler* material.

The boat yard which once consisted of one man and a boy is now big business. Sailing has made the grade. It is all good money-making material. The *Tatler* goes hand in hand with the Jaguars in the village street and a good bank balance.

The dead are for forgetting.

You walk past the house which my father built in 1937. It was a flat piece of land then. Now the garden, to quote the agent's circulars, is "well-matured."

You peer through the thick hedge like a traveler peering up at the walls of a lost city. Those can't be the trees which you planted with Mark?

"I wouldn't have bought this piece of land if I had been Pa," you remember yourself saying.

"Why not?"

"It's too damned flat."

"He's spent a lot of money trying to unflatten it," Mark laughs.

"Trust Pa. A sunken rose garden and a waterfall connected to the mains."

"He never does things by halves."

Mark finishes digging the hole for the macrocarpa.

"Here, you spread the roots out, while I shovel the earth in."

"Let's hope we stay here long enough to see the trees grow." You hear the echoes of your own voice, a voice much younger than it is now.

A sudden shadow crosses his face in the sunshine.

"Let's hope so," he says.

In the road there is the sound of a bicycle bell being rung incessantly.

"Ice cream! I could just do with some!"

Mark leaves me holding the tree, while he scrambles down the rough bank, and through the gate into the lane.

Holding the tree? You look up at it—it must be over twenty feet high. Holding *that* tree? It seems as if it must have been a dream.

You peer again through the garden gate trying to imagine the garden when it wasn't well-matured. Yes, you can just see them —the hydrangeas which your mother brought down from the Sloane Street flat, and they now form almost a barrier round the house.

And there it is, the board, which your father had made so long ago. A nice thick oaken board fixed over the front door, a board into which are cut the words:

"God bless thee friend, be thou but kindly of heart, and thou art welcome."

That board was an embarrassment to Mark. He felt it was a bit corny. Not perhaps quite the thing to put over the door of a week-end cottage.

He pulled a rueful face when my father's workmen put it up.

"A bit of God-wottery," he said.

My father looked hurt for a moment, but he stuck to his guns, his board, and his words. He stuck to them because they were his. He had made them up himself. And there they were going to stay. And there they still are. Still blessing visitors of kindly heart. Perhaps they think it is a piece of God-wottery, perhaps they smile, perhaps they are touched, and have, if only for a few moments, the kind heart their author wished for them, and which he had himself. And which, in spite of his rude remarks about the motto, Mark had, too.

You look into the garden again. Again the double vision of the film "dissolve" assails you. The trees shrink and once more you see the family sitting on the lawn. The hedge, now a dozen feet high, shrinks to a series of tiny separated bushes. The lawn, not so smooth then, sported a set of croquet hoops.

Mark and my father were both people who liked winning when they played games. Their logical minds could see no point in playing games if you didn't win. The object of the game was to win. Anyone with a spark of Gallic blood knew that.

Croquet is not perhaps the best game for people of this temperament. Even the most hardened Anglo-Saxons cannot watch with impunity as their cherished and carefully placed ball is croqueted, not only off the lawn but on to an adjacent field.

Mark and my father discarded any suggestions that Drake was one of their ancestors. They threw down their croquet mallets, they accused one another of cheating, and often the game broke up in disorder. Angry voices came clearly out of the past, angry voices full of deep affection for one another. But was that the lawn where they quarreled? It looks too smooth to have ever been used for such a stormy game. And how could a croquet ball have been "bonked" through that thick hedge?

You look at the drive. It is smooth and well kept. Was that the drive where Mark used to throw down his bicycle when he came in from sailing? The drive where my father used to circle in, driving his Buick with a flourish. He did it once too often, crushing Mark's bike to a mass of twisted metal. You remember your father's furious face as he picked up the bits from under his juggernaut wheels.

"Why can't you put the bloody thing away?" he asks furiously, when Mark comes back from sailing.

"It's too late now," says Mark, "either to ride it, or to put it away."

The voices, one angry and one laughing, come back from the past.

You look at the front door again. It is heavy oak studded with

153

nails. It stood open then and the pram was on the terrace near the sitting-room window.

Mark looks into the pram.

"I don't think babies are at all ugly," he says. He looks at the child in the pram with a humorous, affectionate look. You remember the telegram he sent when the baby was born. "Glad child of superior sex. Mark."

"That's only because *you* know it's the superior sex," you say later.

"That's it. He can crew for me when he grows up."

It was summer then, in 1939, and in half an hour the Walls Ice Cream man would ring his bell. In 1943 it was winter and Judith was saying, "I always knew he wouldn't come back, it was only a question of how and when."

I didn't answer. I couldn't. I went upstairs and reread his last letter. It was sent from the Victoria Hotel, Barrow-in-Furness, and the telegraphic address was Comfort Barrow.

"I have for some unaccountable reason a feeling of intangible sadness around me today. My whole being is spent of emotion as though I have the premonition of some really depressing happening. Life these days seems so pointless and when one gets a little insight into something better—like some good music or a lovely painting—you feel that there is so much more out of the world than in it. But why does one feel so? Maybe I'm being prepared inside for something that I don't want to lose—it can't be my life because I don't give a damn for that."

But it was.

The day after the letter came we all went to Mass. Went to Mass to pray for the safety of the brother, whom the sisters knew was dead, and the son, whom the parents hoped was still alive.

That was ironical. That was a grisly modern joke. Four people kneeling in church reading the familiar words of the missal.

"I go unto the Altar of God, unto God who giveth joy to my youth . . ."

I looked at my father. His eyes were bent to his prayer book, and I remembered walking across St. James's Park with him. We stood at the foot of the war memorial near the Horseguards.

My father read me over the words, "And those who would have been their sons, they gave, their immortality."

I remembered us standing there in the wind, in front of the memorial. Neither of us had then thought that my father would have to give exactly that, his son, his immortality.

Now he humbly knelt in church praying for the safety of his son who was dead. And his faith was not shaken.

Jane's Fighting Ships is an awkward volume. It doesn't seem to have been made to go into a bookshelf. Obviously planned to lie on a table, surrounded by charts, it wasn't made to be kept for a souvenir. It's old and stained now, one of those things which should really have been taken away by the dustman long ago. Sometimes found in a cupboard, sometimes on the floor, it is seldom opened now.

A small slip, with a curiously old-fashioned air, is attached to the 1940 edition of *Jane's Fighting Ships*. It says:

"It is regretted that owing to enemy action affecting the premises of both the publishers and the blockmakers, not only is the date of the publication of *Fighting Ships* considerably later than usual, but it has been found necessary to dispense with two or three new illustrations."

They minded about delays in 1940. A bomb on the premises inconvenienced readers and users. It was regretted.

It was regretted as the death of my brother was regretted by their Lordships of the Admiralty.

15 ✿ ✿ ✿

The Guillotine

I FOUND the guillotine, turning out the cellar last week. It is an instrument for cutting the edges of photographs. It's a bit rusty, but it still works.

It reminded me very forcibly of my father, and his liking for gadgets. He had a quality of whole-hoggery towards gadgets, for he never spoiled any hobby or pastime for the sake of an extra fiver, or even two fivers. If he was going to do a thing, then he would do it properly and hang the expense.

He was a man of sudden enthusiasms, but they were generally enthusiasms which cost money. When an enthusiasm was upon my father, he gave it full reign, like Mr. Toad. Anything new fascinated him. He liked to be in the forefront.

When he was first married, my father suddenly became interested in cars. His brother was in the pioneer car trade. But a car was a little beyond my father's range, so he bought a motor bike. Naturally, he did not only buy the motor bike. He bought a sidecar, a complete leather outfit to ride in, a pair of goggles and a set of maps. He was very fond of maps.

CHEAPEST IN THE END

Those were the spacious days when man was really free. There were no bureaucratic details like driving tests. The salesman showed my father the controls. He got onto the motor bike and drove off, with my grandfather in the sidecar. My mother had prudently taken herself off by train.

It was as well, as it turned out, because beyond Reigate they ran into a brick wall. No one was injured, but my father was justly incensed against the motor bike. He didn't feel that people should sell things which could unaccountably go off the road like that. My grandfather, mistrusting both my father's temper and the motor bike, continued his journey by train. My father, determined not to be conquered by an inanimate object, however mechanically propelled, had the damage repaired. He then tamed the machine into bending itself to his will.

Once my father had bought the motor bike he got a gypsy complex. He was an incurable romantic. Roads weren't crowded long ago. He had the motor bike, and so he felt that he was well on the way to becoming one of the roving kind. He decided that camping was the thing.

Of course, once he had decided on the idea of camping, he needed the right equipment for it. He bought a tent, he bought a special mallet for hammering tent pegs in, he bought a stove, he bought a special set of saucepans to go with the stove, he bought a huge hamper which was full of crockery and table silver. He bought folding beds, bed linen, and he even bought a safety hurricane lamp to hang outside the tent. Knowing my mother's habits, he bought a folding canvas bath for her. He knew that she would not forego her daily bath even in the glades of the New Forest.

He saw it all. He would wake up in the morning. The birds

would be singing. The sunlight would glisten through the branches of the age-old oaks. A gypsy's life, that was the best way to live. My father was happy about the whole thing. He checked over his equipment. There was nothing missing for the life of a real rover.

There was only one item my father had forgotten. My mother. If there is one thing which my mother is not keen on being, it is a gypsy. Or come to that, a rover either.

The nearest thing to being a rover which my mother enjoys is a large luxurious bedroom with an adjoining bathroom, and a view over Paris or the Mediterranean. She has always said that if she can't be really comfortable she would rather stay at home. I can't say that my father had good rover material in my mother.

She did not grumble. She just pointed out a few of the difficulties. While she was cooking, three cows came into the tent. My father explained that they were gentle beasts, and just curious. He was inclined to treat the whole thing as a good country joke, the kind of incident that regularly happened to rovers. My mother wasn't interested; she just felt that cows should know their place, and it wasn't in her tent. Not that she felt her own place was in a tent either. She was gradually beating up to putting that point of view to my father.

After I was born my father was induced to forget camping for a bit. But when I was two or three, the fever came on him again. If my mother had not liked camping *à deux,* she liked it even less with me as part of the equipment. By this time, my father had thought it rather fun to join a camping club. He fondly imagined that my mother would find it amusing to have companions to share the outdoor fun of the roving life.

If my mother didn't like camping, she liked the look of a posse of fellow campers even less. They finally put her off. That, and the fact that I fell in the river.

My falling in the river finally saved the day for my mother. She put her foot down. The roving life was over. My father didn't really mind. He had got a bit bored with the whole thing himself. Besides, the equipment was getting old. He sold it to some other people who had developed a roving streak.

"You'll love it," said my father. "Waking up in the morning, hearing the birds singing."

My mother left the room. She had no desire to spoil my father's sale of his roving equipment. If he kept the equipment, the fever might easily hit him again.

In the early twenties my father was one of the first to own a radio. His greatest chum, the man who had shared digs with him before he married, owned a pioneer radio company. My father became fascinated by radio.

He had a small study devoted to radio. There were seven pieces of large equipment linked by innumerable wires. Getting a program was a considerable feat, entailing as it did getting the seven pieces synchronizing. This required split-second timing. My father would dash up and down, turning knobs. Most of the time the seven-piece conglomeration gave a loud penetrating whistle of protest, but just occasionally the set-up clicked into place.

"Paris!" said my father dramatically. A strange gabble came out of the assembled equipment. We looked into the room awestruck.

Those were the days before the B. B. C. On one epic occasion my father's friend spoke into the apparatus. He spoke to my sister. Out of the mess of coils came the epic words, "Hello, Suzanne."

Just fancy, we all said, he's speaking from Deptford.

Naturally, as soon as radio became standardized, foolproof, and much cheaper, my father lost interest in it. There was no longer any spirit of adventure in the thing. When getting Paris entailed dashing up and down the room forcing synchronized sounds out of sinister black boxes, then a rover could take an interest in it. Once the thing seemed to be really working, there didn't seem to be any point in it. He left it to his children.

He returned to photography.

Photography was an intermittent passion of my father's all his life. The graph of my father's passion for photography was in inverse ratio to the difficulty of taking photographs. He liked it in the early days, when you had to go about with a damned great box, a piece of black-out material, and a folding tripod. When it became easy, and all you had to do was to click a knob, he gave it up. But when, in the thirties, Leicas, light meters, and a new set of complications cropped up, he took it up again. There was fun and adventure in photography once more. There were light filters to be purchased, opposition from clouds to be coped with, and a general air of uncertainty about, with difficulties to be overcome. Then it seemed to be the kind of hobby which it might be worthwhile to pit one's wits against. After all, look at the things which could go wrong.

Once my father had purchased the most expensive Leica he could find, with its satellite light meter, it occurred to him that further fun could be had by developing and printing one's own photographs.

"After all," he said to me, "supposing I take a photograph

and there's just a section which I think would make a picture
—then I can do it exactly right *myself*. You can make photography a real art in that way. There's nothing mechanical about
it."

He looked pleased and enthusiastic.

There was certainly nothing mechanical about the way my
father printed his photographs. In his flat in Sloane Street there
were two bathrooms. He needed the biggest one for his operations, which were of the total variety. He needed total blackness, so he had his carpenter make him a big black screen which
fitted over the window with no chink of light showing. He
also needed total concentration, and he needed total lack of
interruption.

In the bathroom he incarcerated himself, surrounded by porcelain dishes of chemicals, baths full of pure water, clothes pegs
from which hung dripping negatives. There, in a Stygian atmosphere broken by the glimmer of a single red lamp, he performed his miracles.

Most men with hobbies seem to be able to take them quietly.
They plod along gently, enjoying them, and if other members
of the family like to cast an occasional eye over them, they are
content.

My father was not like that. His hobbies were like a whirlpool, they sucked in passers-by. He didn't feel that other people
should miss the fun that was going on in the bathroom. He was
fascinated by developing and printing processes, and he didn't
see why other people shouldn't be fascinated too.

He soon had my two sisters washing negatives, and focusing
his enlarger: he had, of course, decided to buy an enlarger by
this time. After all, there was absolutely no point in wasting

money getting other people to print and enlarge things when you could do it so much better yourself.

"You get the real fun out of photography when you do your own enlarging," said my father. Fun was an oversimplification.

When you get three people moving about in total darkness, amongst the hazards of baths, washbasins, bidets and lavatories, the whole bathroom seems to get a bit tight about the hips.

"If you're not flaming well interested," I heard my father cry out of the total gloom, "why in the hell did you offer to help?"

Suzanne did not reply. There did not seem much point in pointing out that she had been told to help. My father forgot little details like that when he was really interested.

Below the red lamp bad language rose with the fumes of the chemicals. Judith took the opportunity to creep out from behind the bidet. She did not come back.

The thing that annoyed my mother about my father's photography was that it followed her around.

He would issue happily from his playground like some shaggy dog from a noisome pond. And his entrance into the drawing room would have the same effect. Holding dripping prints or negatives in his hand, he would move happily over polished floors and Persian rugs, dripping acid as he went. His progress was interrupted by shrill cries and protests from my mother.

"You're not damned well interested!" he said one day. "You'll like it all right, when the blasted things are finished and dried! You'll be interested then all right!"

He glared at my mother. She did not reply. She was in her lofty mood. He gave her an angry and disappointed look, and then, without speaking, disappeared into the direction of the kitchen.

Here he let down the clothes airer, took down any clothes which were drying, and then, using clothes pegs, pinned all his negatives to dry. The fact that drippings from the ceiling did not make cooking and preparing vegetables an easier task did not concern him. He needed somewhere to dry his negatives. Women were not imaginative. They provided nothing but constant interruptions to a man's little pleasures in life.

He surveyed the lines of dripping negatives, and returned to his Aladdin's cave. My father became aware that his assistants had disappeared for good.

"No staying power," he muttered. "Not ruddy well interested."

He returned to his developing sadly.

Suzanne was expecting a friend for dinner. She was a South American girl who had been at finishing school with her. The kind of South American to whom a trip to Venezuela or Chile rates like a day return to Brighton. It's sometimes difficult to keep up with one's old friends.

When I called round on my way home to my own flat, my mother was dispensing sherry in the drawing room. The finishing-school friend was dressed for dining out, in a Paris dress and one of those thirties hats with little bits of jet and a veil. She was undoubtedly a very pretty girl. She gave me the benefit of a few snacks off her social calendar, a short itinerary of her Grand Tour of France and Italy, and touched lightly on her forthcoming trip home to Venezuela.

"You ought to go to South America," she said.

"Yes, I must go some time," I said. I was wondering if I had the cab fare home.

THE GUILLOTINE

My sister was a long time changing. Time marched on. I showed the finishing-school friend down the corridor and into the bathroom.

I flung the door wide.

A furious face lit by a lurid red light confronted us over a bath of acid.

"Shut that bloody door," said my father.

The girl took a step backwards.

She had had a sudden glimpse into a world less refined than her own. A world where no holds were barred. After one brief horrified glance, she backed away from it. The balance of mind of the very rich is easily shattered. A nasty peep into real life disturbs them. I wasn't really surprised.

My father frightened me even when he wasn't lit up like the demon king.

We didn't see her again.

"Just as well," said my mother. "She kept her hat on at dinner."

I've been puzzling out that remark for the last twenty-five years. Does keeping one's hat on at dinner indicate some deep form of vice which I haven't heard about? I'm not very good on obscure vices and one doesn't like to appear a fool in mixed company.

My father still maintained that photography was a hobby which the whole family enjoyed.

It's a good thing no one goes in for developing and printing in our family now; we've only got one bathroom.

16 ✿ ✿ ✿

The Chinese Plates

THE man who said, "one good turn deserves another," had a twisted sense of humor. What he forgot to add was that the person who did the first good turn was also in direct line to do the second good turn.

Take my father for example. He once met a down-and-out outside the National Liberal Club. He gave the man a job, and the result was that the down-and-out got chummy with one of his female employers. The association proved fruitful. The result was that my father had to find some parents for the fruit of it, and a new job for the woman.

No one could say that my father was deterred by the outcome of some of his good turns. Just as he wasn't letting priests put him off God, he wasn't going to let his neighbors put him off doing good to them.

But sometimes he became temporarily disillusioned. Then he went down to consult his private oracle.

The ancient Greeks, whenever they wanted a bit of off-the-cuff advice about life, took the next litter to Delphi. My father's private oracles were two nuns who lived behind bars, shut away from the world. They were extremely cheerful nuns, and a great stand-by for my father. He drove down to see them whenever he had a row with his fellow directors. This was fairly often.

He also went down to see them whenever his children seemed to be acting foolishly. This was not infrequent, either. He became, in fact, one of their most constant visitors.

I have never found out how my father came to get to know his two convent friends. What advice they gave the stormy character who confronted them through their grille I have no idea. Perhaps they just calmed him down. That would have been quite an achievement, however much the power of prayer, fasting, and contemplation had fortified their spirits.

In return for good advice from his nuns, my father gave them scraps of French brocade to make into vestments, he repaired their roof, he sent men down to see to drains, boilers, and driveways. This was the one case where one good turn really did deserve another. Henri IV said, "Paris vaut une messe." My father reckoned that a prayer merited a refrigerator.

I don't know if his nuns advised him in business matters. But he certainly kept them posted. If they didn't appear in the balance sheet, they ought to have done. They were the backroom girls.

After the war ended, my father came back from one of his usual visits to his nuns. He had been worried about postwar restrictions on his business. But now his brain had cleared completely. He was in no doubt as to what to do.

He bought a Rolls Royce.

"Why a Rolls?" said my mother.

"Going into the shipping business," said my father succinctly. "I've got to keep the factory going."

We agreed, of course, that there was absolutely no sense in going into the shipping business looking as if you needed the order.

Perhaps the nuns had inspired him to buy a Rolls. Anyway, they couldn't have been against it. Especially not as it enabled him to go down to see them more often. When he did, he drove back with the boot filled with homemade jam and pickles and boxes of apples and pears.

We benefited indirectly from the shipping business, because at week-ends we were driven about in a grandly gleaming Rolls with a uniformed chauffeur, giving an entirely false impression of great riches. It was odd to see the contemptuous Socialist looks we got. One longed to get out and explain that the Rolls belonged to the firm. Quite a lesson that you should never trust in appearances.

Naturally his firm did get into the shipping business, and started to make money. There is nothing quite like the gleaming bonnet of a Rolls for winning friends and influencing people.

"You can't pick it up if you don't put it down," said my father.

There was only one trouble with this axiom, as far as my father was concerned. He was inclined to put down his own money. It is well known by those who gamble in large sums that the whole point of departure should be that one never uses one's own money. That way lies bankruptcy.

This was a lesson my father never learned. As soon as the

firm started to make money, he started to spend it.

The return of what is known in the city columns as "consumer goods" to the shops was to my father like the sound of grapeshot to an old war horse. He was making money. Now was the moment when it could be spent.

He bought a huge washing machine, he bought a vast fridge of immense dimensions. To these he added the biggest combined radio and record-player he could find, and, as he now had a posse of grandchildren, he needed a new camera to photograph them. He also needed a television to keep them quiet.

There was something about my father which seemed to attract children. Where once he had been surrounded by his four children, he now had four grandchildren.

Once my father's daughters had grown up and married, they baffled him. He was not interested in the complications of life. Living, to him, was an essentially simple business. Once he had children round him, this point of view was confirmed. Besides, his grandchildren gave him further reasons for spending money.

There's always something a child wants, and where there was a grandchild, there was my father prepared to gratify the child's slightest whim. A Haroun Al Raschid with a Rolls Royce, prepared to drive off to Harrods and stretch all the toys in the world in front of dazzled eyes.

Did his grandson express the wish for a boat to sail on the Round Pond? Presto, a boat appeared. The fact that it was over four feet in length and needed some negotiating to get across Kensington High Street on a special trolley did not occur to my father. The child wanted a large boat and the child got a large boat. The pleasure which was seen for a split second in the child's eyes was enough. Everything else was irrelevant.

"Ridiculous, buying a child a boat that size," said my mother.

My father gave her a look which indicated that women had no breadth, depth, imagination, or generosity of spirit.

My father's feelings about women varied according to whether they were getting in his hair or not. When they were amusing, intelligent, pretty, and agreeing with him, then they were on his level. Once they started to put up a stiff opposition to him, then, like some sudden slide on the Stock Exchange, their value diminished.

Children never let you down, children accepted life as it came. They didn't remind you about your overdraft. They were enthusiastic about new things just for the things themselves. My father had the same childlike enthusiasm. He was enthusiastic about everything he had and did. He was enthusiastic about his children, his grandchildren, and he was especially enthusiastic about his business. His firm was the best firm in the world. They turned out the best work, they bought and sold the best antiques, and he didn't mind whom he told about it.

This enthusiasm was an embarrassment to my mother. She had none of my father's uninhibited feeling for spreading the good news around.

When the war ended, my father celebrated it by having his entire flat done up. He swopped out his antiques for better ones, he had designers in to replan his furnishings, he bought special silk in France for curtains. He really went to town.

And when he had finished he gave a big cocktail party. It seemed a pity not to have a party in such a very nice setting.

He wanted people to see it.

In the middle of the party my mother sailed into the drawing room. She found my father engaged in a serious conversation with one of her friends. He was enthusing about his bureau bookcase.

"Your father is the limit," she said to me. "I really think the poor woman thought he was selling her the bookcase."

"Of course she didn't," said my father. Then he looked at my mother in a humorous way. "Even if I had sold it to her, I expect I should be able to find a better one."

My mother put on a governessy expression. She was not amused. There were things about my father which she didn't find in the least funny.

It was about this time that good antiques began to get a little short. My father decided to put his undoubted talent for sheer buying into antique buying.

He always said he knew nothing about buying antiques. He left that to the experts, he said. He did in fact know a great deal about furniture. He had not been in the business for thirty years for nothing.

My father's antiques expert was a tall, thin man. He looked like one of those old Buddhas which people used to have on mantelpieces. He had the same expressionless face, the same high cheekbones, and the same capacity for nodding his head without expressing any audible opinion. As a buyer or seller he was a great success. His expression gave nothing away. It remained utterly blank. Looking at his face, you couldn't tell whether you were getting a bargain, or whether the piece before you was something which he wanted to move out of the showroom as quickly as possible.

My father loved him. He loved the fact that his antiques buyer could go to an auction and, without moving a muscle, pick out the pieces he wanted, and get them for a bargain price.

"Never gives an inch or an ell," said my father delightedly.

The fact that his antiques buyer adopted the same policy towards his managing director didn't worry my father. You had to take the rough with the smooth.

I often made forays out into the country with my father, after the War. We went in the Rolls. It was amusing to go on expeditions which entailed buying, just for the love of buying. We bought in bulk. We bought chests of drawers, Dutch cabinets in marquetry, leather-covered pedestal desks, bow-fronted cabinets, break-fronted sideboards, and then we would grandly order them to be packed carefully, and sent up to London.

The buying of antiques is a ceremony. It has perhaps the feeling of some rite. Only those who know the rite get the real pleasure out of it. There is the arrival at the shop. An inspection of the terrain is carried out. A casual glance is given through the window. If this casual glance reveals that the quality is up to standard, an entrance is effected. It is useless to bustle into an antiques shop and say that you have come to buy. That is the approach of the amateur.

You stroll in. You throw a glance round the shop. This glance indicates that you are prepared to be amused by some little piece or other. At first blush you don't seem to see anything which pleases you. Once this approach has been indicated, then the antiques seller bustles forward, and the first move is complete. From your approach you have already indicated that you are no dope in the worm-ridden depth of antiques-buying. He knows you merit respect. Now starts the real business. He indicates his bargains. They are usually the things he wants to get out of the way because they are taking up too much space.

There was nothing nicer than poking about in antiques shops with my father. He really got good value out of it. Even when he had expressed willingness to be interested in certain pieces, there was still good value to be got out of the sale.

Negotiations would start. Were the handles original? My father and I would peer inside the drawers. We never seemed to find anything which told us anything.

"I've got something I know you are going to like," said the antiques man on one expedition.

"What do you think about the legs?" My father looked at me. We both inspected the legs of the cabinet in front of us. My father was uncertain about them.

"They don't look right to me," said my father. "I've never seen such heavily carved legs on a simple cabinet like that. I wonder."

My father never gave his enthusiasm full rein when he was buying antiques. He knew when he didn't know. And he knew that his antiques buyer was sitting like an old spider in his office ready to cast disparaging eyes over the results of the expeditions.

We looked at one another. The Buddhalike head of the antiques buyer with his narrowed eyes seemed to be present.

The antiques seller reappeared from the back of his shop. He was carrying a large pottery figure. He set it down proudly on the top of the cabinet. We looked at it in dismay. It was a large fat Buddha. There was no doubt about it, it seemed to be saying no.

"I don't think I'll take the cabinet," said my father.

"What about the sideboard?"

My father gave a side glance at the Buddha. It still seemed to be saying no. My father shook his head again. The man looked a little downcast.

"I'll take the small mahogany desk," said my father.

The man didn't look too happy about it. My father gave me a clandestine wink. The mahogany desk must be a bargain.

"And that pair of tables—did you say you'd let me have them for twenty-five?"

"Thirty."

My father didn't agree or disagree. His eyes traveled up the wall. "What about the gilt mirror?"

"Ten, if you take the tables."

"Very well," said my father, "forty for the pair of tables and the mirror."

"Perhaps your daughter would like these Chinese plates?" said the man.

"How much?"

"Three pounds."

"I'll give you thirty bob," said my father.

The deal was concluded.

"I should take the plates with you," my father said to me. He called out to the man, "My daughter will take the plates with her; it will save you packing them."

My father made out a check for his purchases. The man seemed pleased. As I carried my Chinese plates out of the shop, my father turned to me.

"I thought he seemed a bit too cheerful, didn't you? I wonder if we could have got the tables any cheaper?"

I called in at my father's office the next day. I was having a look around. I needed some dining-room chairs. I pushed open the heavy oak-studded door and went into my father's office.

"How were the things we bought?" I said.

My father laughed.

"I asked Smith about the tables and mirror," said my father. "He said 'Oh, they're all right.' I asked him if they were genuine. He just nodded. Later on I went into the showrooms. I saw the mirror marked at fifty guineas and the tables at sixty pounds."

"So you did get a bargain?"

"I think so. I think Smith thought it was a fluke. He doesn't like to think I know anything. I don't really."

At this moment the heavy door opened again. In came Smith. If he had been wearing a silk robe he couldn't have looked more oriental. He was holding a chair in his hand. It was a rather nice Regency chair with a rope back and a horsehair seat.

"What do you think of that?" he said with no preamble.

"Very nice."

"Bought four of them, only fourteen pounds," said Smith. "Small auction, people haven't got the idea about Regency yet."

"How much did you say?" asked my father.

"Fourteen pounds."

"They'll just do for my daughter," said my father. "She wants some bargain chairs."

It was the only time I ever saw Smith's expression change. Although it would have been an exaggeration to say that his face fell, you could say it slipped a bit. His eyes narrowed. He went out without saying a word. He looked back resentfully.

CHEAPEST IN THE END

What on earth was the use of looking impassive at auctions if one's managing director was going to give the results away, and without a profit?

We still have the Regency chairs, and I must say they were a bargain. We haven't been able to match them. And when we sit on the Regency chairs, we often eat fruit off the Chinese plates. They were a bargain, too.

17 ✿ ✿ ✿

The Bun-Faced Portrait

No one likes the portrait of me in the red dress. They all say it makes me look bun-faced. The general opinion about my face is not unanimous. There are those who are for it, and those who are against it. But all combine to agree that the quality of bundom is something it lacks.

However, I shall continue to defy public opinion and keep the bun-faced portrait. It was painted by a sweet man who is now dead. He was showing my father how to paint. They wanted a model, and so I sat for them in the red dress. Even that looks a bit peculiar now because of the padded shoulders.

When my father retired, or, to put it more correctly, was forced to retire, it was a shock to him. He had never visualized retiring. He had always talked of "dying in harness." The prospect of living in a small house or flat had never occurred to him. The prospect of living on a small income had never occurred to him, either.

He had always been the world's optimist. Next year was always going to be the best year ever. And then suddenly there was no next year, but only a series of years with the same income. No excitement and no more battles. It was a bit flat.

He let his rather grand flat in Sloane Street furnished and went down with my mother to Stratford-on-Avon to look after his grandchildren for the holidays. They were staying in a small comfortable hotel because my sister was working in London.

My father was living in a limbo. He had some idea of helping to get a friend's building business on its feet. He was not going to be idle. After all, he was only seventy-one.

The blow fell rather quietly.

My mother telephoned to say that he had had a stroke. He had been taken to the hospital. The doctors said that it wasn't a bad stroke. He would recover. As it was an emergency, he had been put in a public ward; they might be able to move him later.

The first sight of my father gave me a terrible shock. From being a vigorous, attractive, elderly man, he had suddenly become old. His whole expression seemed to have disappeared. It hung down, as if the side of a cliff, previously rocklike, had turned out to be sand after all. The stroke had not affected his speech, but his brain moved slowly. In the ward another old man, who had also suffered a stroke, shuffled forward, pushing a chair in front of him. Like an elderly baby pushing a toy horse, learning how to walk all over again. I could hardly look at the old man.

It seemed horrible that my father, who had been so good-looking, strong, and all-commanding, should be reduced to lying immobile amongst such poor shattered wrecks. I was embarrassed for his plight. I did not know what to say.

"I've bought you a few pears. The grapes weren't very nice.

We're looking forward to your coming home."

This was the way one talked to fools and dolts, not to my father. I suppose the terrible feelings in my heart were partly caused by a sense of the humiliation he must have been feeling.

After a while we left the ward. The nurses made practical starchy sounds about his recovery. To them he was only the "stroke in bed 3." To us, he was a husband and father who had been struck down. Like a great oak tree, he had sheltered us all, and suddenly he was nothing. Just an old man in a bed who spoke with difficulty.

I remembered him once saying to me that a wife was "a young man's mistress, a middle-aged man's companion, and an old man's nurse." It had seemed a rather harsh Gallic view of life when he had said that to me. I found it faintly disgusting. Yet it was in fact exactly the story of his relationship with my mother.

He recovered from the stroke. But he was crippled. His Savile Row suits, the suits of the managing director behind the eighteenth-century desk in the Georgian room, hung on him. He used a stick.

But he recovered. He was still alive. Alive enough to find his male nurse a dolt and a fool.

I have always thought that people make a great mistake to treat the sick and children as fools. The fact that they are temporarily helpless doesn't affect their brains. They are often much sharper than their keepers. Watch the eyes of the sick, and of children when they are treated like fools. They tell you quite a lot about what they think of their companions.

My father was brought home to the flat my sister had taken. He was amongst his family and he had someone to shout at.

He was quite determined to get better if it was only to get rid of the male nurse. The male nurse seemed an inoffensive little man. Soft-spoken, and did crochet work in his spare time. I've still got the tablecloth the male nurse crocheted. Inoffensive— that wasn't the way my father saw him. Just to spite the male nurse he got better, and sacked him.

It was obvious that my father would now be an invalid. But he got well enough to go out for walks. He could walk as far as the church or the shops. He liked reading thrillers, mostly Peter Cheyney. He who had once tackled St. Thomas Aquinas found it difficult to concentrate on anything which was too hard to understand.

Often when I went into the flat in the afternoons I would find him asleep in his armchair. The large radio was playing so loud that one would have thought the walls of the sitting room would cave in. Fortunately, he was deaf in one ear, found it soothing, and slept like a baby. On the table beside him was his Bible. It was a battered Bible, in the Douay Version. I used to pull his leg about it being the Douay Roman Catholic Version. Once, I asked him if he thought the Authorized Version would corrupt him.

"No," he said, looking puzzled, for there were some things he didn't find amusing, "but this is the right one. I find a lot of good things in it. Solomon had a lot of wise things to say."

His Bible was often open at some comforting paragraph. It's odd really that it is only now that one realizes how difficult it must have been for him to be an invalid. I suppose one lives from day to day trying to help in physical ways, and one gets used to the fact that a man who was intelligent and quick has become old and slow. One just does one's best in small ways, trying to ignore the main fact as if it were something which should not be mentioned. Looking back, one wonders if it was right.

It was about this time that we all decided that my father ought to have a hobby. I remembered how he had liked copying pictures when I was a child. He had copied very ordinary things, the kind of things which people laugh about now. Madonnas with white veils, the Laughing Cavalier, Kirchner pin-ups from World War I, and girls wearing black silk stockings, pulling the wings off cupids. When he was young he had had a great talent for copying different textures. He painted always in water colors, and yet the flesh gleaming through the girls' stockings was touchable and the cupids' wings softly feathery.

So we found an artist to give him painting lessons. My father went with my mother, stumping along with his stick, and bought paints, easel, brushes. There was no good stinting it if he was going in for painting.

The artist was a charming man, and they had a lot of fun together. Sometimes the artist painted, and my father watched. At other times the artist would watch and my father would paint.

My father's uncle had been an artist, and his mother was a great designer of patterns for lace, or ideas for embroideries. Like many Frenchmen he had always been intensely interested in painting. He was never much interested in landscape. Heads and character studies were the things he mostly appreciated. He always had an excellent eye for a picture without ever having studied painting. One day, in his heyday as an interior decorator, he had caught sight of a head of an old man in a millionaire's house. He stopped in front of it.

"That's a good picture," he said to his designer.

"It ought to be," said the designer, "it's a Rembrandt."

This did not disconcert my father. He was not concerned with the current art values. He had thought it was a good picture. And he'd been right.

So when he came to paint in his invalid days he concentrated on heads. Heads of his family. His son who was dead. His granddaughter who amused him. He copied his old Madonnas, with less sureness now, and in oils because it was not such a difficult or delicate medium as water colors.

My father's paintings were stiff. I thought they had that rigid quality which one sees in the portraits painted by Branwell Brontë of his sisters. But although they lacked the professional swirl and sweep of his teacher's hand, they had something which the artist's pictures lacked. They had a likeness.

The bun-faced portrait, painted by the artist, is much less like me than the rigid amateurish picture which my father painted at the same time.

He enjoyed painting, and when he was concentrating on it his face seemed to come more alive. But it was a strenuous hobby for an old man who was sick. He got tired. He found it difficult to concentrate for too long.

I don't want to give the impression that my father was a saintly old man. His halo was far from in evidence. My mother had a great to-do with him every time the doctor wanted to put him on a diet. That really did annoy him. It was bad enough trying to get a good square meal, well cooked, in his present situation, without the doctor interfering, and putting him on some damn fool diet which tasted of nothing.

Another thing they tried to do was to put him off cigarettes and make him smoke a pipe.

"God Almighty!" he would roar, "what have I got left?" My mother never replied. She had always thought Clemmy was inclined to be unreasonable. He hadn't changed.

Occasionally I got the idea that it would be nice for my father to have a drive in the country. I can honestly say that the game wasn't worth the candle. Getting in and out of the car caused swearings, cussings, and a general air of fury. I admit that the car was neither large nor luxurious, but by the time I had got my father into it, I was under no illusions about his opinion of it.

I occasionally used to get romantic ideas of taking my father on a picnic. "A day in the country," I would say to my mother, "he would enjoy that!"

It was a major operation. Try finding some flat ground where you can pitch a chair for a heavy man in the middle of a wood in Sussex. A chair which will remain upright while you serve out lunch. It's not an easy assignment, especially not when your choice of situation turns out to be unfortunate. My father was not one to suffer fools gladly, and if I turned out to be a fool, he was not suffering me gladly, either.

My father still retained an interest in his firm. He had some shares in it which hadn't paid a dividend for years. Once in a while his successor in the managerial chair used to come and see him. Partly, I think out of kindness, and partly to explain why they hadn't made any money that year. My father would have liked to sell his shares. The trouble with these shares was the same as the trouble with most shares—when they aren't making any money no one wants them, and when they are, you don't want to sell them. So no one wanted my father's shares. They had been bought mostly so that he might perhaps have a controlling interest in the firm. Now they only represented a debt to the bank.

The other business interest my father retained was my sister. She had by now a good job in a large firm, and every evening she came home to recount the day's doings and machinations to him. He enjoyed that. It was like the sound of battle to an old war horse. His eyes would light up. He would proffer advice. He would make suggestions on tactics and development. And they were good suggestions. Human nature doesn't change even if the sign over the door has changed from father to daughter.

When it became obvious that my father would never recover sufficiently to have a home of his own, my mother decided that the best thing to do was to sell the lease of the flat, which had been let, and store most of the furniture. She could not quite bring herself to part with everything yet. And we thought that it might be a good plan if we bought a big house in the country and divided it into two flats. My father could then have his own things round him.

The tenants moved out of my father's flat and we went to look at it for the last time. The dining room with its elegant eighteenth-century furniture, the family pictures on the wall, the drawing room with its pale silk curtains, the Regency mirrors, the bureau bookcase reflecting back the light, my mother's bedroom with the crackle-painted furniture and the chintz in white and russet tones—it all looked as elegant as ever. My father stood in the hall looking round. It was like a lost kingdom.

My mother was bustling round arranging this and complaining about that. She was determinedly cheerful. It was no good crying over spilt milk. As she came out of her bedroom he took her hand awkwardly, because he had to hang on to his stick. He raised it to his lips and he kissed it, very gently, very elegantly, like a *jeune premier* of the period when he too looked like one.

I turned away.

My parents were not given to demonstrations of affection even in my childhood.

With that one gesture, it seemed as if he were apologizing that things had not turned out better, that he had not been able to keep her home for her, that he was old and ill, and no longer capable of entering the lists on her behalf.

She smiled at him. He had always done his best. There was no cause for reproach. She accepted his caress, and then she bustled off.

My father watched her go along the passage. He turned and saw me standing in the doorway. He smiled, and looked after my mother again. His eyes traveled to her feet.

"It always gives me a shock to see the kind of shoes your mother has to wear now," he said. Then he looked up at me. "But you won't say anything to her, will you?"

We found a house in the country. Well, not country, Surrey. It was a big Edwardian house. I can't say that it was the house which either of us would have chosen, but it had two huge drawing rooms, and plenty of space for two families to get away from one another.

The garden was large and full of apple trees, and it was level. We started to turn the servants' hall into a bedroom for my father because it was on the ground floor.

In the middle of the move, he had a coronary. But we weren't worried. He had been very ill many times since his stroke. We had had so many fusses and worries, it did not seem to be any different.

The day before we moved was his birthday. He was much better. He was looking forward to the move. All his children and grandchildren brought him presents. The kind of presents he liked. Peaches, pears, grapes, bottles of wine, and French cheeses.

I went in to see him. He was sitting up in bed, propped up. He said he liked his day nurse. She was a good-looking redhead. He had always rather liked redheads, he nearly became engaged to one once, he said, but they weren't too reliable.

I was glad the nurse was good-looking. My father did not like ugly people. It was a strange weakness with him. He had been known to sack a secretary because she was plain.

"How did you like the wine?" I asked.

"Very good. I haven't finished it yet."

He looked at me. I don't know why, but I was always embarrassed with my father when he was ill. There was some barrier between us. A lack of spontaneity. It wasn't that we weren't terribly fond of one another. But we couldn't get through with a demonstration of affection.

"How is it in the country?" he asked.

I knew he was looking forward to living in the country.

"Chaos," I said.

"The garden must look nice on such a lovely day," he said.

"Yes."

The idea of Falstaff, babbling of green fields, flashed through my mind. I dismissed it.

"You'll be able to come down as soon as we have finished your room," I said.

He smiled at me. He was thinking of the garden in the country. I looked at the night table. There was a dish of grapes and peaches, the bottle of wine, three-quarters full, his rosary, and the old battered Bible—Douay Version.

"Goodbye."

I didn't kiss him. I don't know why. I couldn't bring myself to. I felt embarrassed. I just stood in the doorway and blew him a kiss. It was the last time I ever saw him. He died the next morning.

He died before we finished his room, before we had arranged his pretty furniture suitably, or he had seen the cobwebs on the lawn in the September sunshine or the crab apples scarlet on the trees, as they had been in the garden at Copyhold, long ago, where he had commanded gilt chairs on the lawn for my wedding. It was a pity, really.

He died the day after his birthday with the grapes and the bottles of wine still on his night table. His Irish nurse put his rosary in his hands after he was dead. My sister and I drank the wine. My father would have thought it a pity to waste it.

Now when I look back on the progress of his decay and his death, I realize something which I hadn't realized then.

In his sufferings he never complained against Fate. He was never angry with God. And he had learned two things which he had never learned in his pride and strength. He had learned patience, and he had learned humility.

A few days ago, I was speaking to my daughter about my

father. She said to me, "You know what Pa taught me. He taught me faith. I remember one day going into his sitting room. He looked up at me as I ran in from school. I asked him what he'd been doing while I had been away. He looked up, and said that he had been painting Our Lady, and saying his rosary."

Suddenly I had the picture in my mind of the old man, as he was then. My eyes filled with tears.

"It was all right," said my daughter. "One day he was a powerful man with a Rolls Royce, and the next he was—a friend with a stick."

Her voice was full of love and gratitude.

18 ❧ ❧ ❧

The Relic

DEATH always comes as a surprise. It astonishes. We use old phrases like "here today and gone tomorrow." They don't mean anything. And suddenly they are the simple truth.

We had moved down to the country, and before the cases of books were unpacked, before the pictures were hung, the phone rang.

My husband came into the bedroom. It was full of early September sunshine.

He looked at me. For a moment he didn't speak.

"I'm afraid—your father is dead."

I was glad he had used no euphemism. Dead is dead. No softer word can change the fact. My father was dead. In truth he was here today, and on this tomorrow, he was gone.

There is something strange and special about losing one's father. One's childhood is suddenly gone.

My father was old and ill; it was inevitable that he should soon die. And yet, while he still lived, he seemed to have authority. You could ask his advice, and in flashes, he would still be the man he was. The man who did not suffer fools gladly. The man who had intimidated priests into giving him absolution. The man who loved to see his family round a well-laden table. Now he was no longer here.

I looked round the room. Everywhere there were boxes, muddle, chaos. Two electricians were at work. Called, like some music hall act, Ron and Len, they kept popping out in unlikely places through floor boards. They were alleged to be rewiring the house, only they hadn't finished in time. Here and there, where they left little piles of wires, ends of cotton waste and nails, they indicated the presence of something going on underneath, like worm casts on the lawn.

Odd how one's mind focuses on some particular point like that. These wire casts depressed me. I could not speak. My husband took my hands.

"I'll have to go up to London," I said.

He nodded. "I'll carry on here."

I put on my best black suit. It seemed a respectful thing to do. I know that people today don't believe in mourning, and yet as wedding clothes are an outward sign of inward happiness, so mourning is an outward sign of inward sorrow. Sorrow is no shame.

People contend that mourning clothes are a sign of hypocrisy. They are also a reminder of mortality. People don't want to be reminded of that.

I sat in the train. Quite suddenly, family affairs were my responsibility. I was the eldest. I was the one who should be relied on. The first thing to do, I felt, was to make a list of things to be done. So I wrote:

1. Ring for priest.

2. Ring up undertaker.

3. Put notices in the *Times* and *Telegraph*.

I looked at the list. It seemed a short program after his long and stormy life. When I was a child we had learned the Seven Corporal Works of Mercy. We used to rattle them off parrot-wise. The last one was "To bury the dead."

There is a terrible moment of recoil in the face of bereavement. As I stood on the threshold of the flat, I felt a tremble of fear in my heart. For neary fifty years my parents had been married. Fifty years since they had set out, on just such a sunny autumn day, for Paris and their honeymoon. And now the journey was over. She was alone.

I raised my hand and rang the bell. The redheaded Irish nurse opened it.

"He died very peacefully," she said, "no pain." And then she added comfortingly, "I've put his rosary beads into his hand. Do you want to see him?"

I shook my head. There didn't seem to be any point. She looked at me again.

"I thought you had better have this," she said. She handed me his gold watch. It was a square gold watch with an expensive movement. There was no use in buying badly when it came to buying watches. The most expensive was the cheapest in the end.

I made some movement of surprise.

"You never know with the undertakers," she said darkly.

I took the watch. My father had been a stickler for time, and it had rather a large secondhand. The kind of secondhand which could indicate that a person had been kept waiting at least half a minute.

CHEAPEST IN THE END

I thanked her and went in to my mother. She seemed a little smaller. I am no great believer in equality for women. A woman is a complementary thing and a woman alone is diminished. She falls into the background. She is already the past.

I kissed her. She cried a little, and then she said, "I always prayed that he would have a peaceful death."

The redheaded nurse brought in the inevitable cups of tea.

Cups of tea which are used to fill the empty spaces of sadness. Cups of tea which are not used for refreshment, but rather as a means of occupying one's hands.

The bell rang.

"That'll be the priest," said the redheaded nurse.

She said it as one would say, "That'll be the milkman." There is a great comfort about the Irish. They take birth and death as part of a great cycle. It must be sad to be surrounded by atheists, when death creeps softly into a family.

I went into the hall. The priest was a tall fresh-faced man. He had often brought my father Communion when he was ill. My father hadn't liked him. He thought him a bit of a fool, but then that was my father's opinion of most people.

"I'll just go along and see him," said the priest, as if he were paying a visit to an old friend. Presently he came back. The prayers for the dead had been said. The practical details had to be approached.

"I expect we'll have to get on to an undertaker," I said.

I was suddenly conscious that as head of the family all the arrangements were for me to make.

The priest looked at me, astonished. His face told me that these were not the kind of duties usually taken on by women.

"Haven't you got a brother?" he said.

"No. My brother was killed in the War."

He looked embarrassed, as if his slip had made the thing a social solecism.

"Never mind," I said. I felt sorry for him. It was not his fault that my brother had been killed in the War.

"I'll ring the undertaker," he said.

The consolations of religion have pecuniary rewards. When the undertaker came he was a nice little man, with a professionally solicitous manner. We discussed the quality of coffins.

"Perhaps we should have the best oak," I said. The best is always the cheapest in the end. And this was an end.

"Give me the address of the chapel of rest," I said. "I'll have some flowers sent round."

Another theory is that flowers don't do the dead any good. But like the black of mourning, they do honor them.

The Irish maid was crying in the kitchen. She probably felt that everyone was taking the thing too calmly. A little Celtic gloom, she felt, would not come amiss, and she was the one to supply it. While I was talking to the undertaker she came in.

"The night nurse is here."

"What does she want?"

"She didn't say."

This gave rise to a fresh outburst of sobbing from the maid. I went out before we had a real scene out of O'Casey.

The night nurse stood in the doorway to the flat. She was a prissy person. My father hadn't liked her. If he had managed to live another couple of days, he was going to sack her. I wasn't surprised. She had a disapproving look. The kind of look which suspects that the drains aren't working any too well.

"I hear the patient died," she said. She expressed neither surprise nor concern.

"Yes."

"I've come for my things."

"Come in and get them," I said, with a vague wave of my hand in the direction of the room where she had been sleeping.

She looked at me again, still disapprovingly.

"Here's my account," she said, producing a crisp envelope.

I looked at her. I could have given her a check then and there. But suddenly I was angry. Angry that she should be so lacking in feeling, that her bill should be the only thing uppermost in her mind, that, to her, my father's death meant no more than ten guineas owing, that she should stand there like the broker's man, demanding her due, with my father's body lying in the next room.

"Thank you," I said.

I put the bill into the pocket of my black suit. Might as well keep her in suspense. Let her worry for a few days whether she was going to have to apply to lawyers for her money. Lawyers always took a long time.

I turned on my heel and went back to the undertaker.

"One final thing," I said to the undertaker. "The notices in the papers."

"*Times* and *Telegraph,* of course," he said. It was like the repetition of a chorus.

"Of course," I said.

"Perhaps you will write out what you want to say," said the undertaker helpfully.

I wrote out a simple death notice, and handed it to the undertaker.

He looked at it dubiously.

"I shouldn't put the address in," he said.

"Why not?"

"It's the secondhand clothes men—" he said.

I fingered my father's gold watch in my pocket. The red-headed nurse had warned me about the undertaker's men, and now the undertaker was issuing a warning in his turn. There is a gruesomely farcical side to death.

"Very well, leave out the address."

The idea of a posse of secondhand clothes men fingering my father's suits did not appeal to me. Burke and Hare still have a few old chums left.

When I was a child at school we often had a Dead Mass, with the orange unbleached candles standing round the catafalque, and the silken pall arranged as if there were a coffin underneath. There was no coffin, it was only November 2, All Souls' Day.

But this September day, at Mass, under the silken pall lay my father's coffin, and the unbleached candles indicated mourning for his death. I knelt beside my mother, my sister, and my husband, and behind me was his grandson.

The great familiarity of the words of the Mass seem to bestow on grief the solace of formality. A formality which gives a pattern to the progress from birth to death.

"We will not have you ignorant concerning them that are asleep, that you be not sorrowful, even as others who have no hope."

One must always have hope, even in death, when the coffin under the catafalque is that of your father. My mother did not cry, either. She is not fond of demonstrations of emotion. Emotions are for concealment.

CHEAPEST IN THE END

When the Mass was over we filed out into the sunshine. We paused on the steps. I suppose we looked an ordinary, rather drab little procession. There was nothing terribly grand about the funeral of a man who had dwindled away into death. There was no pomp. No blast of trumpets, only the undertaker's men taking the coffin towards the hearse.

An official of my father's firm came up to me.

"Don't worry about your mother's pension," he said. He looked upset. It was something to say.

I wasn't worried about my mother's pension. It was the result of my father's last fight with his board.

I looked out into the sunshine of the road. The undertaker's men were arranging the flowers in the hearse. My mother's sheaf of roses was on the coffin itself.

My husband took my mother's arm.

"Better you shouldn't come to the churchyard," he said.

"I'll come," said my son.

"There's no need."

"But I want to." He did not make an emotional speech. He just wanted to be there. His grandfather had been a friend.

The four of us got into the funeral car.

"You know what I was thinking of in church," said my sister. I shook my head.

"I was thinking of Pa in Massetts—cutting the lawn."

The sunshine of long ago echoed in her words. Sunshine in which we were all much younger.

Soon we were standing at his graveside. Two daughters, the son-in-law who was the only one of my young men he had tolerated, and his grandson. I hoped we justified the confidence he had always had in us.

THE RELIC

Above the open grave the sky was the delicate blue of early September, around on the grass lay great mounds of flowers.

It was a beautiful day. The kind of day it must have been when my father was born. Born the son of a French refugee.

Dust to dust.

The priest passed us all the holy water in turn. We sprinkled it on his coffin as it slid out of sight.

I was glad that our son was there. It was good to see him sprinkling the holy water. It represented continuity. Continuity and a sense of gratitude for the past which had been beautiful.

My sister looked down into the grave. She was interested to see how deep it was.

We thanked the priest. It was over.

"I'm glad it was such a lovely day," said my sister.

Nuns are great hands at making something out of nothing. My father's favorite nuns had enclosed some earth from the grave of Ste Thérèse of Lisieux in a scrap of silver brocade. I have attached it to the card which tells me the number of his grave. The grave is a little difficult to find because it is a large graveyard.

I went there one day last spring. The municipality plants it with flowers for us. It was quite an enjoyable visit. I got very chatty with a couple of spinsters who were energetically weeding near the Catholic section. They showed me the right path.

They were weeding rather angrily. They confided to me that they were not weeding one of their own graves. They would scorn to own such a grave. The weeds annoyed them. How dare anyone let a grave get into such a mess?

I felt a little decadent paying the Council to do my weeding and planting.

I put my flowers on the grave. As I regained the path towards the gate, the spinsters greeted me cheerfully.

"See you here again," they shouted gaily.

That's really it. We shall all be seen there in the end.

19 ❧ ❧ ❧

When the Saints Go
Marching In

MY father was a man of great imagination and limitless optimism. While his imagination enabled him to plan projects and make money, his optimism caused him to spend too prodigally. Like his grandfather, the gentleman with the heavy-lidded eyes, whose portrait hangs in our house, he left nothing to me of value. Nothing of value, that is, except two saints. It is not everyone who inherits two saints. It is a unique legacy.

The two saints live according to a harsh rule formed in the sixteenth century. Their dress is coarse and darned, they never eat meat, and their convent is unbelievably cold; even when the spring sunshine is warm outside you can feel this cold eating into your body as if it were some slow form of medieval torture; and in this cold they wear rope-soled sandals, with uppers of linen which they can slip into wooden pattens when they work in the mud, outside in their vegetable garden.

Their house was given to them by the relict of a chocolate

manufacturer. It is an ugly house of late Victorian pretentiousness, all gables and curlicues; a house of moderate proportions with ideas above its station. To it are attached a coach house and stables much too large for the house itself.

This is the only part of the house which can be seen by visitors. In winter the short, back drive to the coach house is covered in dead brown leaves, which swirl up to the chapel door and clutter the gutterings of the gables.

You ring the rickety bell which hangs on the wall, and presently a woman appears. The two saints are dependent upon a pair of hands and a pair of feet for shopping and contact with the outside world, which they have not seen these thirty years.

You go up a short flight of stairs, so steep that it is an effort not to slip on the polished wood. Your stiletto heels make a loud echoing noise and you turn the corner into a completely bare room. Two chairs neatly set out for the visitors wait expectantly.

In front of them is a window covered in black painted bars from which protrude, on the visitors' side, spikes about four inches long and as thick as a finger. Behind the bars, brown shutters. A small amount of light falls from a high window, a dim glow comes from a small oil stove which does little to break the penetrating cold.

Soft footsteps, the shutters open, and there are the two saints, happy to see you, congratulating you on your new hat and the soft fox on your thick winter coat. It is a compliment to the two saints to wear your best clothes.

Presents are exchanged. Sugar, tea, tinned fish are put into the intercommunicating drawer, which is pushed forward, and the saints take out the presents which, by now, seem rather in-

WHEN THE SAINTS GO MARCHING IN

adequate and trivial. And then the two saints put their presents into the drawer, which is pulled backwards.

You take out pots of pickles, jams, and spiced onions, each neatly labeled with its date, a little cross, and the letters A.M. D.G.—Ad Majorem Dei Gloria—for pickles, if well pickled, can be offered for the greater glory of God.

The exchange of presents then leads to the exchange of news. They hear of triumphs and setbacks, gossip and scandal, births and marriages.

What is their news? Strangely enough, it is so often of frustrations and difficulties.

Saints, it seems, are not in general demand.

The busy world finds them something of a burden, for they are poor. On paper they are an administration problem, for their house is old. It needs repairs. The Urban District Council casts its eyes on its dilapidated Victorianism. Better that it should be swept away.

Ideally, of course, the saints should live in the forest of Arden, where wild beasts would gladly give them fur for winter warmth, and bees would leave honeycombs under their eaves.

But the world which the saints have forsaken is crawling like some primeval monster towards them, making threatening gestures.

Their sad, old-fashioned garden is flanked by a row of modern flats with television aerials; their little chapel bell is drowned by the roar of lorries and cars along the new by-pass. This by-pass has already sunk its teeth into their garden, and bulldozers have felled some of the bank of trees which kept them protected from the eyes of the world.

And now, say the saints, the Council is making threatening

gestures again. Official letters are being written. Compulsory purchase is being mentioned. The Council has powers. Which means Power. The mailed fist of modernity is held above the frail Victorian villa, and there casts its shadow. The garden, where the daffodils still bloom under the apple trees, is threatened with leveling and with the concrete mixer. Tall blocks of flats will march across the orchard where the convent cat now plays. The crab apple which makes such delicious jelly —A.M.D.G.—will go for firewood.

Progress is all. The majority must be right.

For what good is a saint? Or worse still, two saints?

They can appear on no balance sheet—*upkeep of two saints: £200 a year.* They can't be written down—*depreciation on two saints: £150 a year,* or *fair wear and tear on saints: £10.15.0.*

What would the tax inspector say if you were to approach him and demand agreed expenses for the maintenance of two saints?

"Saints? Saints? Let me see."

He would take down a large volume of tricky tax problems. Here under the letter S are impaled the hopes and fears of many, but this is the final word. He would allow upkeep of saxophones for jazz musicians, security guards for bankers. Farmers could charge for seed, chemists for scales, jockeys for saddles. There were allowances for sales, sanctions, safes, salaries, and sanitation.

"Nothing, I'm afraid," he would say with a grim look. "Nothing under saints—your charge will be disallowed." Perhaps he would add, "What business are they in?"

You would confess that their sole means of support was the making of wafers for communicants, and the stiff gold embroidery of the chasubles of priests, or the copes and miters of bishops.

You would see from his face that, in the great world of the export drive, these were commodities which were little in demand, and did not greatly benefit the sterling area.

"What do they live on?"

"Charity."

"If they are *registered* as a charity, then they can claim the return of tax paid on agreed income signed under a covenant."

It would seem a dusty way of supporting a saint.

But the television aerials which peer over into the sad, winter garden of the saints will never reflect their image, or vote them top personalities for 1962.

Their worn black breviaries are unlikely to be chosen Book of the Month. The cars which throw their exhaust fumes over the remaining trees in the garden of the saints are unlikely to organize a Saints' Rally in their honor. Workmen cycling home from factories are unlikely to stop and leave a grateful loaf at their door. There are few alms for the love of God.

The Council will propose no vote of thanks to them for honoring the borough with their presence. The age of television is not the age of saints and scholars.

Saints are an anachronism. The great broom of progress will sweep them away.

The last time I saw my two saints was on a sharp day in December. My sister took them a hamper. They seemed a little older, a little more resigned. But their faces had no lines of discontent, only a beautiful slow resignation of spirit. They complained that their fingers were slower over the embroidery and their movements stiffer in the garden and kitchen.

It's hard to be old, even when you are a saint. They were still worried about the Council. The fist hung poised, suspended.

The day drew in, the cold crept closer till it was a living thing. Soon, because there was no electric light in the room, the faces of the saints glimmered in the reflection of the rising moon as if they were already transfigured.

It was time to go. My sister found that she had forgotten to give them the white chrysanthemums which she had brought for the altar.

They were carefully placed in the drawer. Goodbyes were exchanged, and the last we saw of the saints were two veiled black figures handling the enormous white flowers which glowed incandescently in the December darkness, like the promise of perfection.

We left them alone in the black, cold darkness, handling the moonlike flowers.

The roar of the traffic soon shut the sound of their voices out of our ears, but the dark, Spanish picture of the veiled figures and the white flowers remained in our minds.

The bus was full of chattering children from the Secondary Modern School which flanked the garden of the saints. Could you ask them to get up a Save the Saints Fund?

"My father's on the Council—he says we can't have *saints* in the borough."

"Saints? Whoever heard of anything so soppy?"

But the age of miracles is not quite past. The saints do have friends, though death has taken their main benefactor, my father. A doctor, a journalist, an actor send them occasional help. A friendly solicitor has stayed the concrete fist of the Council.

WHEN THE SAINTS GO MARCHING IN

The saints live in the limbo of the modern world—the building reprieved, but only reprieved, from an Order for Compulsory Purchase.

The saints are old, and the moloch waits in the wings. The jaws of the mechanical grab wait to drip with the red earth. Action is only postponed.

What use are the lives of these saints?

They are cold, they are hungry, they are poorly clad. And they are old. Yet when they lift their heavy black veils, their faces are often amused and gay, alert with interest. Locked away, imprisoned in cold, their minds are free.

The sins which swirl about in the dark world—lust, divorce, betrayal—the sadness which drifts over happy lives, the loss of youth in war, the gradual decay of the strong, to all these tales from the outer darkness they bring a warm living faith and a human kindness. Never condemnation.

The saints are tired now.

They write that they are preparing for a journey, they have received extreme unction. Yet one still hopes that they will live to see the cat playing amongst the flowers in their spring garden for a little while.

You ask me what good are my saints? I can only answer: they are good.

But if it should not be ordained that they should see the spring again, if it should be that their journey must be undertaken, then one should hope that the "Saints Will Go Marching In" to the sound of loud triumphant trumpets and clad in the cloth of gold that they have so often stitched for the glorification of others. So let the Saints Go Marching In to the light of the sun.

20 ❧❧❧

The Legend

WHEN I was a child my father would tell me fairy stories. He had a good histrionic feeling for them. He had the knack of conjuring up a great world of fantasy and strangeness, the kind of world which frightened and enchanted a child. His bears would roar frighteningly, and would show fierce white teeth. His princes would be tall and dignified, more beautiful than anyone ever seen on earth.

Sometimes he liked to pop in a little moral to the story, enchanted when the point of the story had been taken by his captive audience.

This was one of his stories.

In the days of legend, there was, of course, the usual prince. He was young, he was brash, he was very sure of himself. He set off from his father's palace, full of dreams of princesses, fortunes, crocks of gold, grand friends, glittering raiment, chargers caparisoned with shining armor—in fact, all the average things which most young princes have their heads full of most of the time.

He journeyed through terrible hazards. He was attacked, sometimes by wild beasts, sometimes by men in the shape of beasts. He journeyed through terrible darknesses. He was betrayed, and sometimes he betrayed. Many times he lost hope. Many times he lost faith. Many times his heart was full of hate. At the end of his journey he came once again to his father's palace.

He found him dying. The prince knelt at the bedside of the old king to catch his last words.

"I have left you a great treasure," said the old king, and he fell back dead.

The young prince wondered what the treasure could be. Was it the palace, the land which surrounded it, the river full of shining fish, or the forest full of springing deer? What could it be?

As soon as the old king had breathed his last, in came the creditors. They took the palace, they took the land, they took the river full of shining fish, and the forest full of deer. He watched them loading the old king's treasures on to carts going to the market. The creditors were laughing. They had reason to. For there is nothing like getting treasure at good rock-bottom prices which will make a profit.

"Where is the treasure which my father left for me?" asked the young prince.

"There's nothing except this box," said the creditors, and they handed it over. It would fetch nothing, it was made of cracked deal.

The young prince opened the box, and inside he found a piece of dusty parchment.

On the parchment was written, in his father's neat hand, these words, "Honesty, Truth, Firmness of Purpose, and Endurance."

The young prince was very angry. How dared his father waste his substance, put himself in the hands of his creditors, promise him a fortune, and then leave him nothing but a piece of paper?

He made his way through the porters carrying out the wonderful furnishings of the palace. He threaded his path through the men loading them onto market carts, out onto the highway where the creditors sat in their glittering carriages. Their faces were smug. This added fuel to the prince's anger.

For some time he trudged along the dusty road and then he thought of an old wise man, a friend of his dead father, a despised friend, for he was poor and unsuccessful.

He made his way through the winter woods to the hut of the wise man and found him sitting by the fire.

The young prince railed against the creditors, against the injustices of his lot, and the evil of the world.

The old man said nothing in reply to the prince's furious outpourings. He was so old that he could only be angry at injustices which affected others.

At last, when the prince had finished, the old man spoke.

"Don't you see," said the old man, "don't you see that you have in your hands the secret of a happy life? For those four words spell integrity."

"That's a fine useful legacy to pay your bills with," said the young prince angrily.

The old man smiled sweetly.

THE LEGEND

"You are quite right," he said, "it is. If you are able to leave as much to your children, you will have achieved something."

I thought it a dull story. Now I am not quite so sure. When you are middle-aged you stand at the crossroads of life. You are able to look back over the past with a tolerant eye, and yet to give a hopeful glance to the rocky ground confronting your children.

You suddenly know the things which are important to you. When I think of my father's life and death, it seems a rounded whole. To each of his children he gave something of himself. To my brother, who died, his courage. To my sister, who sits behind her executive desk, wearing his gold watch, his drive and optimism. To his youngest daughter, working on her remote island in Canada, surrounded by the sea which has taken her husband and three children, his endurance.

To me? I don't know.

Perhaps just the ability to remember with affection.